EXCAVATIONS AT SAQQARA

NORTH-WEST OF TETI'S PYRAMID

by

A. El-Khouli and N. Kanawati

With contributions and drawings by E. Thompson,
N. Victor, A. McFarlane, R. Scannell and H. El-Tayeb

VOLUME II

Published by The Ancient History Documentary Research Centre
Macquarie University, Sydney, 1988 .

ISBN: 0-85837-626-1

Published by: The Ancient History Documentary Research Centre
Macquarie University, North Ryde, N.S.W. 2109, Australia

Printed by: Adept Printing Pty. Ltd.
13 Clements Avenue, Bankstown, N.S.W. 2200, Australia

Distributed by: Aris and Phillips Ltd.
Church Street, Warminster, Wilts, England

PREFACE

The excavations to the north-west of Teti's pyramid undertaken by Macquarie University, Australia, in 1983 and 1984 (see the first volume of the present series) were continued in January and February, 1988 by the Egyptian Antiquities Organisation in collaboration with Macquarie University. The cost of the dig was borne by the Egyptian Antiquities Organisation, while the expenses of the Macquarie University staff participating in the project were covered by the Australian Research Grants Scheme. We wish to express our appreciation to the sponsors for their generous support.

It is a great pleasure to acknowledge the contributions made to our work by various individuals and institutions. Mrs. Elizabeth Thompson (Research Assistant, Macquarie University) helped on all stages of the project, and was responsible for the recording of the architectural details and of the later burials and finds. Mr. Naguib Victor (Maksoud), (Research Fellow, Macquarie University) provided valuable assistance on site and was responsible for the preparation of all the architectural drawings. Field records for tombs, objects and fragments discovered in 1983 and 1984, included in the present volume, were taken by Lady McFarlane (Research Assistant, Macquarie University). Mr. Hasaballa el-Tayeb (Saqqara) and Mr. Reece Scannell (Macquarie University) carried out all the photographic work of the dig.

We would also like to acknowledge the co-operation of the Chairman, Dr. Ahmed Kadri, and staff of the Egyptian Antiquities Organisation, and of Dr. Helayel, Director of Saqqara, and his staff. Mr. Mohamed Bedeir and Mr. Nader Ramadan, Inspectors of Antiquities, supervised the fieldwork and Reis Mohamed Abu-Shehat expedited the dig with his usual energy and care.

As with the first volume of this work, the record of scenes, inscriptions and finds published here in photographs, will, we trust, give the reader an appreciation of the original material. Where no clear photographs were obtainable because of the condition of the monument, line drawings are provided, as in the case of the false doors of Mehi and Ishfi and the central panel of Hesi's door. These drawings were produced from multiple photographs and site records by Mrs. Elizabeth Thompson, who also took charge of the preparation of the final artwork of this volume. In this respect the contribution of the Audio-Visual Services Unit of Macquarie University, and particularly that of Mr. Tan Teong Eng, Ms. Effy Alexakis, Mr. Reece Scannell and Mr. Stephen Ransom is especially appreciated.

Dr. Colin Hope (University of Melbourne) was kind enough to read the chapter on the finds and to offer constructive comments, and Miss Kim Wilson, Miss Jennifer Draper and Dr. Greg Horsley (Macquarie University) patiently and accurately edited the present text.

Finally, our thanks are extended to the Ancient History Documentary Research Centre and its Director, Professor Edwin Judge, for including this report among the publications of the Centre, and to the Rundle Foundation for Egyptian Archaeology for its contribution towards the cost of printing this volume.

* * *

Excavations of the mastabas of Iri/Tetiseneb, Mehi and Hesi, which began in 1984, were completed in 1988. New sections of these tombs were cleared and as a result, some modifications and additions have been made to the General Plan (Plate 1). Digging continued further north, where a new row of mastabas was uncovered, whose rear walls were attached to those mentioned above. These new tombs are, from the east, Mastaba C, the mastaba of Ishfi and a third mastaba, excavation of which was not completed.

From the discovery of a number of intact burials, dating from the Eighteenth Dynasty or later, in the sand (approximately six metres high) above the Old Kingdom mastabas, it was obvious that these mastabas had not been disturbed since Dynasty 18. Yet unlike the mastabas excavated in previous seasons, where nearly all the decorated stone blocks were found *in situ* or to have fallen in the immediate vicinity, none of the three mastabas found in 1988 retained any decorated blocks. However, we are fortunate to have information on Ishfi due to the fact that his entrance lintel and false door were thrown into his shaft and possibly pushed inside his burial chamber (see under the mastaba of Ishfi).

Like most owners of mastabas in this section of the Teti Cemetery, Ishfi was in charge of the *ḫntj-š* officials, and like some of these owners his name and figure were chiselled out wherever they had appeared on the false door (see *Saqqara* 1, 11-12). It is reasonable to assume that the removal of the owner's name, or name and figure, or the mutilation of certain parts of the body of the figure, represent different punishments inflicted upon the owners. We are uncertain whether in all cases the punishment was for their participation in one and the same event. Indications are that the reigns of Teti and Pepy I were not free from internal problems.

The row of tombs discovered in 1988, including the mastaba of Ishfi, is certainly later than the row to its south containing the mastabas of Iri, Mehi and Hesi. The tombs in this newly discovered row were built against the previous ones, using the latter's north walls as a common wall. The alteration of Teti's cartouche on Mehi's architrave and the deliberate change of Tetiseneb's name to Iri on his lintel, which was not possible on the architrave, suggest that both these officials served during the period from the end of the reign of Teti to the beginning of Pepy I, including

Userkare. Neither of these tomb owners, nor Hesi, seem to have been implicated in the events of the period, for no damage is evident in their monuments. On the other hand, Ishfi seems to have lived in the latter part of Pepy I's reign, and if the damage to his false door reflects a punishment, then this could have been the result of his involvement in the conspiracies against this king. One is tempted to connect Ishfi with the events which led to the disgrace(?) of the vizier Rawer (El-Fikey, *Rē-wer,* passim).

A feature of three of the tombs published in this report – those of Hesi, Ishfi and Mastaba C – is the reuse of the mastaba, or part of it, probably by members of the owners' families. However, in no case do any of the original shafts appear to have been reused; rather new ones were cut. This applies to Shaft VIII of Hesi, Shaft III of Ishfi (used by Mesi) and Shaft IV of Mastaba C. In the last two instances, the original chapels were blocked and their main shafts may never have been used, perhaps because of the disgrace of their owners (see under Ishfi). The case of Hesi is different, for the inner room in his chapel may have been allocated to a relative(?), without affecting the offering room or the false door of Hesi himself.

The reuse of old mastabas necessitated the construction of additional walls, which are easily distinguished by the use of darker, smaller mud bricks, irregularly laid and by the frequent addition of pieces of stone between the mud brick, as in the surviving section of Mesi's wall, above Shaft III in Ishfi's mastaba. One may assume that most of these later, more fragile walls had collapsed and that they perhaps once supported the false doors found fallen in the area.

When a later addition to a mastaba clearly resulted in major alterations to its shape, two plans are included: one showing the original design, the second showing the present plan with all the alterations. This was particularly necessary in the cases of Hesi and Ishfi. Sections of shafts and burial chambers are viewed from north or south, depending on the best vantage point from which to show the important details. The viewing direction with regard to individual shafts is indicated by arrow-heads on the plan of the mastaba. The scale given on each plate applies to all plans and/or sections on this plate.

As a rule, our plans are drawn from a height of 1.00m., which seemed the most appropriate point from which most architectural features could be shown on one plan. Sections are drawn for chapels only when enough of the vaults are preserved and are given for shafts where burial chambers occur. In the individual plans of mastabas, only those parts built by the tomb owner are shown in brickwork; a common wall with a previous mastaba is represented by a straight line. False doors, set vertically in the brick walls, appear in hatched lines; thresholds and offering slabs, laid horizontally on the floor, are left unhatched. Because of the small scale of the plans, the panelling of the false doors is not represented.

The present volume includes burials and objects from the Eighteenth Dynasty to the Roman period found in the course of the 1988 excavations, the Old Kingdom mastabas between the third and fourth streets behind the mastaba of Mereruka (see General Plan), and all the decorated fragments found during the seasons of 1983, 1984 and 1988. While the superstructure of the mastaba of Hesi was totally uncovered and the mouths to all the shafts identified, only Shaft VIII was cleared. Work also began on the mastaba to the west of that of Ishfi before the season came to an end.

Ali El-Khouli and Naguib Kanawati

CONTENTS

PREFACE 3
ABBREVIATIONS 6
THE MASTABA OF IRI/TETISENEB 7
THE MASTABA OF MEHI/MEHNES 12
THE MASTABA OF HESI 18
MASTABA C 23
THE MASTABA OF ISHFI/ISHFU 25
THE REUSE OF ISHFI'S MASTABA BY MESI 30
INSCRIBED OBJECTS AND FRAGMENTS 33
BURIALS AND FINDS 42

PLATES

1. General plan
2. The mastaba of Iri/Tetiseneb, plan and sections
3. Iri, architrave and lintel
4. Iri, false door
5. The mastaba of Mehi, plan and sections
6. Mehi, architrave
7. Mehi, false door
8. Mehi, false door
9. Mehi, chapel, false door of Khenti
10. The mastaba of Hesi, plans
11. Hesi, false door
12. Hesi, panel of false door
13. Hesi, chapel, false door of Tetiankh
14. Mastaba C, plan and sections
15. The mastaba of ishfi, plan and sections
16. The mastaba of Ishfi; reuse by Mesi
17. Ishfi, lintel and false door
18. Ishfi, false door
19. Ishfi, false door
20. Mesi, false door and side slab
21. Mesi, false door and side slab
22. Kai, false door
23. Khnumhetep and hesut, false doors
24. Iri, Kedut and Kasedja, offering tables and false door
25. Kedet, Djefti and Pepyankh, offering tables and obelisk
26-40. Fragments
41-49. Burials and finds

ABBREVIATIONS

Ägyptens Aufstieg: *Ägyptens Aufstieg zur Weltmacht* (Mainz am Rhein, 1987).
Alliot, *Tell Edfou 1933:* Alliot, M., *Rapport sur les fouilles de Tell Edfou 1933,* FIFAO, X.2 (Cairo, 1935).
ASAE: *Annales du Service des Antiquités de l'Égypte.*
Badawy, *Nyhetep-Ptah:* Badawy, A., *The Tomb of Nyhetep-Ptah at Giza and the Tomb of ʿAnkhmʿahor at Saqqara* (Berkeley, 1978).
Baer, *Rank and Title:* Baer, K., *Rank and Title in the Old Kingdom: The Structure of the Egyptian Administration in the Fifth and Sixth Dynasties* (Chicago, 1960).
Barta, *Opferliste:* Barta, W., *Die altägyptische Opferliste von der Frühzeit bis zur griechisch-römischen Epoche* (Berlin, 1963).
von Bissing, *Gem-ni-kai:* von Bissing, F. W., *Die Mastaba des Gem-ni-kai,* 2 vols. (Berlin, 1905-11).
Bourriau, *Umm el-Ga'ab:* Bourriau, J., *Umm el-Ga'ab: Pottery from the Nile Valley before the Arab Conquest* (Cambridge, 1981).
Capart, *Rue de tombeaux:* Capart, J., *Une rue de tombeaux à Saqqarah,* 2 vols. (Brussels, 1907).
Céramique, *Cahiers de la céramique égyptienne.*
Cooney, *Glass:* Cooney, J. D., *Catalogue of Egyptian Antiquities in the British Museum, IV, Glass* (London, 1976).
Chron. d'Ég.: *Chronique d'Égypte.*
Davies, *Ptahhetep:* Davies, N. de G., *The Mastaba of Ptahhetep and Akhethetep at Saqqarah,* 2 vols. (London, 1900-1901).
Davies, et al., *Saqqâra Tombs:* Davies, W. V. – El-Khouli, A. – Lloyd, A. B. – Spencer, A. J., *Saqqâra Tombs I: The Mastabas of Mereri and Wernu* (London, 1984).
Duell, *Mereruka:* Duell, P., *The Mastaba of Mereruka,* 2 vols. (Chicago, 1938).
Dunham, *Naga-ed-Dêr:* Dunham, D., *Naga-ed-Dêr Stelae of the First Intermediate Period* (London, 1937).
El-Fikey, *Rē-wer:* El-Fikey, S. A., *The Tomb of the Vizier Rē-wer* (Warminster, 1980).
Firth-Gunn, *Teti Pyr. Cem.:* Firth, C. M.-Gunn, B., *Teti Pyramid Cemeteries,* 2 vols. (Cairo, 1926).
Fischer, *Dendera:* Fischer, H. G., *Dendera in the Third Millennium B.C. Down to the Theban Domination of Upper Egypt* (New York, 1968).
Fischer, *Varia:* Fischer, H. G., *Egyptian Studies I: Varia* (New York, 1976).
Frankfort-Pendlebury, *Akhenaten:* Frankfort, H. – Pendlebury, J. D. S., *The City of Akhenaten* (London, 1933).
Gardiner, *Grammar:* Gardiner, A., *Egyptian Grammar,* 3rd ed. (London, 1969).
GM: *Göttinger Miszellen: Beiträge zur ägyptologischen Diskussion.*
Goedicke, *Königliche Dokumente:* Goedicke, H., *Königliche Dokumente aus dem Alten Reich* (Wiesbaden, 1967).
Golden Age: *Egypt's Golden Age: The Art of Living in the New Kingdom 1558-1085 B.C.* (Boston, 1982).
Gomaà, *Zwischenzeit:* Gomaà, F., *Ägypten während der Ersten Zwischenzeit* (Wiesbaden, 1980).
Hassan, *Saqqara:* Hassan, S. (ed. by Zaky Iskander), *Excavations at Saqqara,* 3 vols. (Cairo, 1975).
Hayes, *Scepter:* Hayes, W. C., *The Scepter of Egypt,* 2 vols. (New York, 1959).
Helck, *Beamtentitel:* Helck, W., *Untersuchungen zu den Beamtentiteln des ägyptischen Alten Reiches* (Glückstadt, 1954).
Hope, *Ancient Egyptian Pottery:* Hope, C. A., *Ancient Egyptian Pottery from the Collections of the National Gallery of Victoria and the Australian Institute of Archaeology* (Melbourne, 1982).
Hope, *Pottery:* Hope, C. A., *Egyptian Pottery* (Aylesbury, 1987).
James, *Khentika:* James, T. G. H., *The Mastaba of Khentika Called Ikhekhi* (London, 1953).
JEA: *Journal of Egyptian Archaeology.*
Jéquier, *Particuliers:* Jéquier, G., *Tombeaux de particuliers contemporains de Pepi II* (Cairo, 1929).
Jéquier, *Monument funéraire:* Jéquier, G., *Le Monument funéraire de Pepi II,* 3 vols. (Cairo 1936-40).
Junker, *Gîza:* Junker, H., *Gîza,* 12 vols. (Vienna, 1929-55).
Kanawati, *Egyptian Administration:* Kanawati, N., *The Egyptian Administration in the Old Kingdom: Evidence on its Economic Decline* (Warminster, 1977).
Kanawati, *Governmental Reforms:* Kanawati, N., *Governmental Reforms in Old Kingdom Egypt* (Warminster, 1980).
Keramik: *Meisterwerke Altägyptischer Keramik* (Höhr-Grenzhausen, 1978).
L.Ä.: *Lexikon der Ägyptologie.* Herausgegeben von W. Helck und E. Otto (Wiesbaden, 1972-).
Lapp, *Opferformel:* Lapp, G., *Die Opferformel des Alten Reiches* (Mainz am Rhein, 1986).
Lepsius, *Denkmäler:* Lepsius, C. R., *Denkmäler aus Ägypten und Äthiopien,* 12 vols. (Berlin, 1849-59); *Text,* 5 vols., and *Ergänzungsband* (Leipzig, 1897-1913).
Martin, *Hetepka:* Martin, G. T., *The Tomb of Hetepka and other Reliefs and Inscriptions from the Sacred Animal Necropolis, North Saqqara 1964-1973* (London, 1979).
Martin-Pardey, *Provinzialverwaltung:* Martin-Pardey, E., *Untersuchungen zur ägyptischen Provinzialverwaltung bis zum Ende des Alten Reiches* (Hildesheim, 1976).
Mélanges Mokhtar: *Mélanges Gamal Eddin Mokhtar,* 2 vols. (Cairo, 1985).
Merrillees, *Pottery:* Merrillees, R. S., *The Cypriote Bronze Age Pottery found in Egypt* (Lund, 1968).
Metropolitan: *Ancient Egypt in the Metropolitan Museum Journal,* vols. 1-11 (New York, 1977).
Newberry, *Scarabs:* Newberry, P. E., *An Introduction to the Study of Egyptian Seals and Signet Rings* (London, 1908).
Petrie, *Scarabs:* Petrie, W. M. F., *Historical Scarabs* (Chicago, 1889).
Petrie, *Amarna:* Petrie, W. M. F., *Tell-el-Amarna* (London, 1894).
Petrie-Brunton, *Sedment:* Petrie, W. M. F.-Brunton, G., *Sedment 2* (London, 1924).
Ranke, *Personennamen:* Ranke, H., *Die altägyptischen Personennamen,* 3 vols. (Glückstadt, 1935-77).
Riefstahl, *Glass:* Riefstahl, E., *Ancient Egyptian Glass and Glazes in the Brooklyn Museum* (New York, 1968).
Samson, *Amarna:* Samson, J., *Amarna, City of Akhenaten and Nefertiti* (London, 1972).
Saqqara: Kanawati, N. – El-Khouli, A. – McFarlane, A. – Maksoud, N., *Excavations at Saqqara: North-west of Teti's Pyramid* 1 (Sydney, 1984).
Schenkel, *Frühmittelägyptische:* Schenkel, W., *Frühmittelägyptische Studien* (Bonn, 1962).
Sethe, *Urk.:* Sethe, K., *Urkunden des Alten Reiches* (Leipzig, 1932-33).
Simpson, *Qar and Idu:* Simpson, W. K., *The Mastabas of Qar and Idu: G7101 and 7102* (Boston, 1976).
Simpson, *Western Cemetery:* Simpson, W. K., *Mastabas of the Western Cemetery:* Part I (Boston, 1980).
Strudwick, *Administration:* Strudwick, N., *The Administration of Egypt in the Old Kingdom* (London, 1985).
Wb.: Erman, A.-Grapow, H., (Edd.), *Wörterbuch der ägyptischen Sprache,* 5 vols. (Leipzig, 1926-31).

THE MASTABA OF IRI/TETISENEB

I THE TOMB OWNER AND HIS FAMILY

The Tomb Owner

NAMES

1 – *Ttj-snb*[1] 'Tetiseneb'. The name appears only on the architrave which was most probably above the entrance to the tomb. It was also written, and later erased, on the lintel.

2 – *Jrj*[2] 'Iri'. This name is repeatedly used on the false door, the entrance lintel and the architrave, where it is once described as *rn.f nfr* 'his beautiful name'.

TITLES

1 – *jmj-r zš* 'overseer of the scribes'.

2 – *jmj-r swt špswt pr-ᶜ3* 'overseer of the noble places of the palace'.

3 – *jmj-r st pr-ᶜ3* 'overseer of the department of the palace'.

4 – *jmj-r st ḫntj-š pr-ᶜ3* 'overseer of the department of the *ḫntj-š* officials of the palace'. The responsibilities of these officials have been discussed in the previous volume,[3] where it was also pointed out that the plural reading of *ḫntjw-š* (and other titles) seems more likely after *jmj-r, sḥḏ*, etc. Here, however, we have attempted to give only the written signs in transliteration.

5 – *wḏᶜ-mdw m swt špswt nt pr-ᶜ3* 'one who judges in the noble places of the palace'.[4]

6 – *ḥm-nṯr ḏd swt Ttj* 'priest of the pyramid – One steadfast of places is Teti'.

7 – *ḥrj-sšt3 n sḫt ḥtpt* 'privy to the secret of the fields of offerings'.[5]

8 – *ḥrj-tp d3t* 'controller of clothing'.[6]

9 – *ḫntj-š ḏd swt Ttj* '*ḫntj-š* official of the pyramid – One steadfast of places is Teti'.

10 – *z3b ᶜḏ-mr pr-ᶜ3* 'judge and administrator of the palace'. The addition of *pr-ᶜ3* indicates, according to Junker, that the holder was a palace official.[7]

11 – *zš ᶜ nswt pr-ᶜ3* 'scribe of royal documents of the palace'.

12 – *smr pr* 'companion of the house'.

13 – *sḥḏ ḫntj-š pr-ᶜ3* 'superintendent of the *ḫntj-š* officials of the palace'.

14 – *špsj nswt* 'nobleman of the king'. As Fischer has already observed, this title is usually combined with that of *smr pr.*[8]

The Family of Iri

A wife(?) and a son(?) appear with the tomb owner on the architrave, but with no names in relief. It remains possible that the names were written in ink which has disappeared.

II DATING OF IRI

The type of false door and architrave,[9] the style of relief, the palaeographic details,[10] the priesthood in Teti's pyramid as well as the name Tetiseneb, all combine to suggest a date in Dynasty 6. The location of the mastaba, adjacent to that of Mehi in the same street leading to the mastaba of the vizier Seshemnefer and close to the latter,[11] leaves little doubt that Iri is to be dated to Pepy I's reign.

III ARCHITECTURAL FEATURES

Pl. 2.

East of the tomb of Mehi and facing south towards that of Iries are an antechamber and a chapel which form the western part of the mastaba of Iri/Tetiseneb. As the east wall of these two chambers lies on the boundary of the concession, excavation was not continued in the eastern part and measurements are therefore incomplete. Presumably the tomb extends eastward following the line of the south wall. There one might expect to find the main shaft of Iri/Tetiseneb and possibly others of his family.

All of the excavated walls are constructed in black mud brick, laid with black mud mortar and plastered. The floors of both chambers are paved with mud brick and coated with mud plaster. There is no sign of any stone casing, but three limestone blocks found in the course of excavations, two forming an architrave (measuring .96m. x .52m. and 1.42m. x .52m.) and the third, a lintel (measuring .51m. long x .12m. high) almost certainly belong to this mastaba. The west wall of the tomb is formed by the thick east wall of Mehi's tomb and is preserved to a maximum height of 1.80m. The façade faces south and against its plastered surface, to the west of the entrance recess, the north wall of the antechamber of Iries is constructed. The remaining walls are all damaged and survive to heights from .80m. to 2.00m. The roofs of the two chambers are destroyed but the construction of a vaulted roof could be assessed from well preserved brickwork in the SE corner of the chapel.

The width of the façade cannot be measured as excavation was limited to that part west of the doorway. This section of the façade is preserved to a height of 1.35m. and includes the western half of an entrance recess. Although clearance did not proceed beyond the eastern door jamb, if the doorway is axial to the entrance recess, as is the case in neighbouring tombs, the width of the recess may be presumed to have been 1.95m. It has a depth of .12m. and shows traces of both mud and gypsum plasters.

The doorway measures .55m. wide x .60m. thick and opens into a small antechamber 1.23m. N-S x .90m. E-W. Although the roof is destroyed, the north and south walls are of a thickness to carry a vault oriented E-W like the roof of the chapel. The use of an unusually thick wall separating the antechamber and the chapel as a support for the vaulted roofs of both rooms may explain the very low height of the doorway in that wall. Fragments of black mud plaster covered with yellow plaster and coated with gypsum plaster are found on all four walls. Three tall, narrow niches of equal size built into the west wall each have a sill height of .45m., the depth and width both measuring .11m. As the wall is partially destroyed, the niches are not complete in their upper parts and are preserved only to a maximum height of .45m. Like the walls of the chamber, these niches also received coats of black mud, yellow and gypsum plasters. The area of the mastaba west of the thick west wall of the antechamber contains a small square shaft.

In the thick north wall of the antechamber is a low doorway, .50m. wide x .90m. thick x .90m. high. It is surmounted by a rough, uninscribed limestone lintel, .80m. wide x .12m. high. At the floor level a small, raised brick threshold measures .10m. thick x .10m. high. This doorway gives access to a chapel oriented E-W which measures 1.70m. N-S x 1.95m. E-W and which originally had a vaulted roof with an estimated ceiling height of 2.20m. The roof is destroyed but the details of its construction are clearly visible in the SE corner where the walls are preserved to a height of 2.00m. All of the walls, except the west wall, still have traces of black mud plaster coated with yellow plaster over which white gypsum plaster was applied. In the centre of the west wall, which stands to a height of 1.70m., is placed an inscribed false door made of a single piece of limestone. The cornice is missing and the present measurements of the door are .69m. wide x 1.45m. high. It is decorated in incised hieroglyphs and may be unfinished, as the sides of the frame show traces of painted black lines indicating that they were intended to be decorated with a banded frieze. The false door rests on an uninscribed limestone platform .75m. wide x .20m. deep x .15m. high.

IV BURIAL APARTMENTS

Pl. 2.

Two shafts were cleared, one in the SW corner and the other in the NE section of the mastaba. The area to the east of the chapel was not fully excavated and would undoubtedly contain other shafts including the main shaft of Iri.

SHAFT I

In the SW corner of the mastaba, west of the antechamber, is a small shaft with a mouth .90m. square. All four walls are lined with mud brick above the rock level, the north wall being formed by the thick wall separating the antechamber from the chapel and the east wall by the west wall of the antechamber. The foundations and the east wall of the tomb of Mehi form the west wall, into which is cut, at a height of .30m. above rock level, a niche measuring .30m. wide x .65m. high x .20m. deep. The south wall is constructed against the entrance wall only to the same height as the floor of the mastaba providing a ledge .30m. deep along the width of this wall. The shaft descends through rock to a depth of 2.60m. At the floor of the shaft an opening in the east wall is 1.00m. high and has a step of .10m. leading down to the floor of a rectangular burial chamber. It measures 2.45m. N-S x 1.50m. E-W x 1.10m. high and lies beneath the antechamber.

SHAFT II

A second small shaft with a mouth .85m. square lies in the NE corner of the mastaba, .30m. south of Shaft III in Mastaba C and .50m. from the eastern wall of the chapel of Iri/Tetiseneb. The shaft consists of an upper section constructed of mud brick with an average height of 2.00m. and a lower section, .45m. deep, cut through the bedrock. It has no burial chamber.

V SCENES AND INSCRIPTIONS

Pls. 3-4.

The architrave, the lintel and the false door are decorated in good quality incised relief with some modelling and details added to the human figures and to some hieroglyphic signs. No colours are now visible. The top of the architrave projects outward, while the top (but not the sides) of the false door has a torus moulding. The cornice, which was presumably formed of a separate block, is now missing.

The Architrave of Iri

Pl. 3.

Holding the staff and the sceptre, Iri stands at the left wearing a shoulder-length wig, a collar, a pendant and a short skirt. Behind him, with one hand on his shoulder and the other holding his arm,[12] stands his wife wearing a fillet and streamer,[13] a long, tight dress, bracelets and anklets. Holding on to Iri's staff and carrying three geese is a small male figure, perhaps a son. Neither his name nor that of the wife were incised, but may have been added in ink which has disappeared.

Six horizontal (1-6) and one vertical (7) lines of text read: (1) *[ḥtp] dj [nswt] ḥtp dj Jnpw tpj ḏw.f ḫntj zḥ-nṯr jmj wt nb t3 ḏsr qrs.t(j).f m ẖrt-nṯr m zmjt jmntjt j3w nfr wrt m jm3ḫw ḫr nswt ḥm-nṯr ḏd swt Ttj Jrj* (2) *ḥtp dj nswt ḥtp*[14] *Wsjr ḫntj Ḏdw prt-ḫrw n.f m wp rnpt Ḏḥwtjt tpj rnpt W3g ḥb Zkr [m] ḥb wr Rkḥ m ḥb hrw nb* (3) *ḥtp dj nswt ḥtp dj Jnpw tpj ḏw.f ḫp.f ḥr W3wt nfr(w)t nt jmnt ḫppt jm3ḫw ḥr.sn m ḥtp m ḥtp ḫr Wsjr n ḏd(.j) nfr wḥm(.j) nfr* (4) *jr jz pn jrj.j m ẖrt-nṯr jn nswt rdj n.j st.f m jm3ḫw ḫr nswt jr(r) ḥzzt nb.f jw rdj.n(.j) ḏb3w n ẖrtj-nṯr* (5) *jr.n(.j) sw r ḥtp.f ḥr.s jw jr.n(.j) k3t jm.f m ꜥwj(.j) ḥnꜥ msw(.j) snw(.j)*[15] *zš ꜥ nswt pr-ꜥ3 sḥḏ ḫntj-š pr-ꜥ3 jm3ḫw Jrj* (6) *ḫntj-š ḏd swt Ttj z3b ꜥḏ-mr pr-ꜥ3 wḏꜥ-mdw m swt špswt nt pr-ꜥ3 . . . špsj nswt Ttj-snb rn.f nfr Jrj* (7) *jmj-r st ḫntj-š pr-ꜥ3 Jrj.* '(1) An offering which the king gives and an offering which Anubis who is on his hill, foremost of the divine booth, who is in the embalming place, lord of the sacred land gives: that he be buried in the necropolis in the western desert, at a very good old age, as an honoured one before the king, the priest of the pyramid – One steadfast of places is Teti, Iri. (2) An offering which the king gives and an offering which Osiris foremost of Busiris (gives). May an invocation offering come forth for him on the opening of the year feast, the Thot-feast, the first of the year feast, the Wag-feast, the Sokar-feast, and [on] the great feast, the burning feast and in the daily feast. (3) An offering which the king gives and an offering which Anubis who is on his hill gives, that he may travel upon the beautiful roads of the west, upon which the honoured ones travel. In peace, in peace before Osiris, for I said what was good and reported what was good. (4) As for this tomb which I made in the necropolis, it was the king who granted its place for me, as one who is honoured before the king, one who does what his lord favours. I made payments to the stonemason. (5) I did it so that he was satisfied about it. I did the work in it with my hands, together with my children and brothers. The scribe of royal documents of the palace, the superintendent of the *ḫntj-š* officials of the palace, the honoured one, Iri. (6) The *ḫntj-š* official of the pyramid – One steadfast of places is Teti, the judge and administrator of the palace, one who judges in the noble places of the palace, the nobleman of the king, Tetiseneb, his beautiful name, Iri. (7) The overseer of the department of the *ḫntj-š* officials of the palace, Iri'.

Iri's explanation of how he built his tomb is of particular interest. The fact that its site was assigned to him by the king is a statement of the obvious, yet it may explain the reason for the unusual similarity in the size of tombs of equal officials at a given time.[16] One would expect that the area given to each official would be governed, in the great majority of cases, by the position he held in the administration. Accordingly, the size of the tomb was a status symbol. However, with few exceptions, the individual paid for the construction of his tomb, the quality of which was determined by his means. Family obligations and private property varied from one individual to another. In this respect, it is interesting that Iri employed only one stonemason, which is clear from the singular determinative after *ḫrtj-nṯr* (line 4) and the suffix *f* in *ḥtp.f* (line 5). This is explained by the unusual statement of Iri that he carried out the work on his tomb with his own hands, helped by his children and brothers. His immediate neighbour to the west, Mehi, employed a number of stonemasons, but he may have been unmarried. The only other person named in Mehi's tomb is his mother, who also owned a false door (see below).

The Lintel of Iri

Pl. 3.

jmj-r zš (jmj-r) swt špswt pr-ʿ3 jm3ḫw ḫr nṯr ʿ3 Jr[j] 'the overseer of the scribes, the overseer of the noble places of the palace, the honoured one before the great god, Iri'. It is curious that the name was originally written as *Ttj-snb,* but was replaced by *jm3ḫw ḫr nṯr ʿ3 Jrj.*

The False Door of Iri

Pl. 4.

The Central Panel: Iri sits on a chair with lion's legs and a low back. He wears a shoulder-length wig, a collar and a pleated skirt. In front of him are an offering table and three stands carrying food, jars of drinks and a ewer. The inscriptions read: *jmj-r st pr-ʿ3 Jrj ḫ3 t ḫ3 ḥnqt ḫ3 p3t* 'the overseer of the department of the palace, Iri, a thousand of bread, a thousand of beer and a thousand of cakes'.

The Lintel: *ḥtp dj nswt ḥtp Jnpw tpj ḏw.f prt-ḫrw n.f špsj nswt Jrj* 'An offering which the king gives and an offering which Anubis who is on his hill (gives). May an invocation offering come forth for him, the nobleman of the king, Iri'.

The Right Outer Jamb: *jmj-r st ḫntj-š pr-ʿ3 smr pr ḥrj-tp ḏ3t jm3ḫw Jrj* 'the overseer of the department of the *ḫntj-š* officials of the palace, the companion of the house, the controller of clothing, the honoured one, Iri'. The owner is depicted with the staff and sceptre.

The Right Inner Jamb: *jmj-r st ḫntj-š pr-ʿ3 ḥrj-sšt3 n sḫt ḥtpt Jrj* 'the overseer of the department of the *ḫntj-š* officials of the palace, he who is privy to the secret of the fields of offerings, Iri'. The owner is depicted with the staff and sceptre.

The inscriptions and figures on the left jambs are identical with those on their right counterparts. The sceptre on the inner jamb is missing.

NOTES

1. Ranke, *Personennamen* 1, 385:10.
2. Ibid, 41:1.
3. *Saqqara* 1, 15.
4. Junker, *Gîza* 6, 211, fig. 83, only written as *n* (not *nt*) *pr-ᶜ3*.
5. For other officials connected with the *sḫt ḥtpt* see *Saqqara* 1, 15, 19 n. 11.
6. Helck, *Beamtentitel*, 66.
7. Junker, *Gîza* 6, 210-11.
8. Fischer, *Dendera,* 98-99.
9. For references to the different types see Fischer, *Dendera,* 215ff.
10. Notice, for example, the use of the determinative ⊗ in the epithet of Anubis *jmj wt* (Schenkel, *Frühmittelägyptische,* 40, 107).
11. *Saqqara* 1, 9.
12. For other examples see Lepsius, *Denkmäler* II, pls. 24, 32, 43, 93d; Hassan, *Saqqara* 3, fig. 33; Simpson, *Western Cemetery* 1, fig. 43.
13. For a similar headdress see Lepsius *Denkmäler* II, pl. 73; Simpson, *Qar and Idu,* fig. 25; Simpson, *Western Cemetery,* fig. 17.
14. *dj* is also omitted after Anubis in the formula written on the lintel of the false door of Iri.
15. The determinative is written once for both *msw* and *snw.*
16. Kanawati, *Egyptian Administration,* passim.

THE MASTABA OF MEHI/MEHNES

I THE TOMB OWNER AND HIS FAMILY

The Tomb Owner

NAMES

1 – *Mḥj*[1] 'Mehi'.
2 – *Mḥ-n.s*[2] 'Mehnes'.

TITLES

1 – *jmj-r ḫntj-š* 'overseer of the *ḫntj-š* officials'.
2 – *jmj-r st ḫntj-š pr-ˁ3* 'overseer of the department of the *ḫntj-š* officials of the palace'.
3 – *smr wˁtj* 'sole companion'.
4 – *sḥḏ ḫntj-š* 'superintendent of the *ḫntj-š* officials'.
5 – *špsj nswt pr-ˁ3* 'king's nobleman of the palace'.

The Family of Mehi

On his architrave Mehi is said to be born to Khenti. A false door in his chapel belongs to a woman named *Ḫntj/Ṯtj*, who could be his mother. On the other hand, the phonetic writing of Anubis on the false door may suggest that this was somewhat later (perhaps only slightly) than Mehi's own monuments (see under Dating). If the false door did not belong to Mehi's mother, it may have belonged to a daughter named after his mother. The woman depicted with Mehi on the panel of the false door is unnamed.

NAMES

1 – *Ḫntj*[3] 'Khenti'.
2 – *Ṯtj*[4] 'Tjeti'.

TITLE

rḫt nswt 'acquaintance of the king'.

II DATING OF MEHI

The date of Mehi may be established with a reasonable degree of certainty. He clearly refers to himself as being honoured before Teti. Since no other king's name is mentioned in Mehi's tomb, one may safely assume that his career, up to the time of building the tomb, was mainly under Teti. Yet the cartouche of this king is inscribed on a separate block of stone, inferior in quality and workmanship. The most likely interpretation is that the name of Teti has probably replaced that of another king whom Mehi also served, but from whom he later wanted to dissociate himself. It seems reasonable to consider that the original name was that of Userkare, the immediate successor of Teti, and that his name was replaced by that of Teti after the latter's son, Pepy I, regained his father's throne.[5]

Other evidence from neighbouring tombs supports the abovementioned deduction. Slightly to the east of Mehi's tomb in the same narrow street, is the tomb of a vizier, Seshemnefer, whose name and figure have been deliberately chiselled out, but whose biography relates his career under Isesi, Unis and Teti.[6] Abutting on the south side of Seshemnefer's tomb is that of the overseer of Upper Egypt, Nikauisesi, who is mentioned in Teti's decree from the temple of Khenti-amentiu at Abydos.[7]

It should be stated that while the false door of Mehi is typical of its period, the phonetic writing of Anubis on Khenti's false door is an indication of a later date. The same writing is attested on the false door of Tetiankh, where the determinative ⊗ was used for the epithet *jmj wt* of Anubis.[8] This determinative was already obsolete by the end of Dynasty 6.[9] The phonetic writing of Anubis was common in burial chambers of Dynasty 6,[10] but did not become usual in the inscriptions of the chapels until the end of this dynasty or later.[11] Suggested date: End Teti – early Pepy I for Mehi, but perhaps a later date for Khenti's false door.

III ARCHITECTURAL FEATURES

Pl. 5.

The mastaba of Mehi is located between those of Hesi to the west and Iri/Tetiseneb to the east, on the north side of the third street behind Mereruka. Its entrance is directly opposite that of Irenakhti on the south side of the street. The mastaba is rectangular in shape, measuring 5.80m. N-S x 4.35m. E-W. The façade, whose entrance recess extends west, gives a total width of 4.65m. to the mastaba. The façade and the superstructure surrounding the shafts are constructed solely of black mud brick, but the east and west walls of the chapel include pieces of limestone. All brickwork was laid with black mud mortar and on the façade are traces of black mud plaster covered with gypsum plaster. A space left between the west wall of the mastaba of Mehi and the east wall of that of Hesi is filled with stone rubble. The south wall shows no clear division between these two tombs, and the entrance recess of the façade of Mehi extends slightly west of the line of its external west wall (as does the burial pit of the main shaft). The south walls of both mastabas would appear to be built as one continuous façade, which suggests the possibility of simultaneous construction. Against the plastered façade east of the entrance recess is built the antechamber of the mastaba of Iries which completely blocks the street. The east wall forms the west wall of the later tomb of Iri/Tetiseneb. All of the walls are well preserved, those in the western half standing to a maximum height of 2.10m., while those surrounding the shafts in the eastern part remain to an average height of 1.80m. The roof is destroyed and no measurements of the vaulted ceiling of the chapel can be provided. The upper walls and roof of the chapel have now been reconstructed in modern brickwork to protect the original chapel.

The façade has an entrance recess 3.40m. wide x .13m. deep which originally had a large, inscribed limestone architrave spanning its entire width. The architrave was most likely formed of three blocks of stone, two of which, measuring 1.38m. x .52m. and 1.19m. x .52m., were found in clearing the rubble and sand filling the street in front of the tomb. Towards the top of the entrance recess at a height of 2.10m. the remains of a shallow horizontal ledge indicate the original position of the architrave.

The doorway, .50m. wide x .80m. thick, does not lie axial to the chapel into which it opens but is contiguous with the east wall. The corridor chapel measures 4.50m. N-S x 1.20m. E-W. Although all the walls of the chapel stand to a maximum height of 2.10m., the details of the vaulted ceiling which rested on the east and west walls cannot be reconstructed. All four walls, as well as both entrance jambs, retain traces of black mud plaster coated with gypsum plaster. At the southern end of the west wall is a small, inscribed limestone false door .50m. wide x .65m. high. All figures and inscriptions are roughly executed in incised relief and the decoration appears to be unfinished, as details of the torus moulding and the cornice are left in black paint. The door is raised .10m. above the floor level of the chapel and possibly had an offering slab in front of it. North of the false door a small niche was built into the brick wall at ground level. The sides taper, giving a trapezoidal shape, the width being .23m. at the bottom and .14m. at the top. The height is .85m. and the depth is .12m. and all surfaces are coated with mud and gypsum plasters. It is surmounted by a small limestone lintel, very rough and uneven, which measures .38m. long x .07m. high. At the far northern end of the wall is the main false door formed of one piece of limestone measuring .68m. wide x 1.60m. high x .32m. deep. It is fully inscribed in incised relief with some details left unfinished and the decoration of the torus moulding barely begun. Under and in front of it is an uninscribed limestone platform 1.15m. wide x .15m. deep x .15m. high.

The eastern half of the mastaba is entirely occupied by three shafts within thick mud brick walls. The main shaft lies directly east of the northern false door in the NE corner. Its thick south wall separates it from a second shaft(?) which was not cleared. The area in which it lies measures 1.35m. N-S x 1.70m. E-W. A wall only one brick thick separates Shaft II from Shaft III which lies in the SE corner of the mastaba. In order to facilitate access to this smaller shaft, a ledge .30m. deep was left in the west wall and behind this, additional brickwork was constructed against the east wall of the chapel.

IV BURIAL APARTMENTS

Pl. 5.

The mastaba contains three burial shafts, one of which was not cleared. The other two were found plundered.

SHAFT I

The main shaft in the NE corner of the mastaba has a mouth 1.65m. N-S x 1.60m. E-W, all four walls being lined in mud brick to base rock. It descends through rock to a depth of 7.65m. where a large burial chamber opens into the west wall. Basically rectangular in shape, it is unfinished at the western end where the west wall is curved with large sections of rock left uncut and where the ceiling is sloping and uneven. The burial chamber measures 3.20m. N-S x 3.25m. (average) E-W x 1.30m. high. All four sides of a burial pit cut into the floor near the west wall are incomplete and uneven. The external measurements of the pit are 2.30m. x .70m. At a depth of .60m. a ledge .15m. deep is left on the south, east and west walls, except at the northern end. The remaining width of .40m. was excavated for a further .40m. to give a total depth of 1.00m. To the east of the burial pit, a complete and cleanly cut lid 2.60m. x 1.15m. x .30m. thick rests exactly on two long, narrow blocks of stone. Laid parallel to each other they are cut to a size 2.00m. x .30m. x .20m. high. The unfinished appearance of the burial pit with its lid still on a stand waiting to be moved into its place over the pit, suggests that the burial chamber may never have been used. Near the SE corner of the burial chamber a niche measuring .95m. wide x .75m. high x .35m. deep was cut into the south wall. The burial chamber lies under the northern false door and extends westward beyond the external west wall of the mastaba.

SHAFT III

The south and east walls of this small square shaft are formed by the external walls of the mastaba. A thin brick wall separates it from Shaft II to the north, while a ledge .30m. deep spans the west wall at a height of .85m. above base rock. A mouth 1.00m. square narrows slightly as it descends to measure .90m. N-S x .95m. E-W at the floor of the shaft, cut to a depth in the rock of only 1.20m. A burial chamber opens to the west, being cut at an angle to give an orientation of true N-S rather than the local N-S alignment of the cemetery, and does not lie under the chapel. It is small and shapeless with an average length of 1.90m. x average width of .83m. x .80m. high.

V SCENES AND INSCRIPTIONS

Pls. 6-9.

All scenes and inscriptions are in incised relief. The execution of the reliefs on the architrave is far superior to that on either of the false doors inside the chapel, Mehi's being also of better workmanship than Khenti's. The reliefs on the architrave show some internal details, but no colours are visible.

The Architrave of Mehi

Pl. 6.

Two, or possibly three, pieces were found. The text, written in seven horizontal lines (1-7), appears to be complete, and the missing piece probably depicted the tomb owner and perhaps members of his family. A small fragment of stone (fragment No. S88:265) on which the name Mehnes is written may have belonged to this third piece. The smaller size of the hieroglyphs on the fragment may indicate a label for the owner's figure, rather than a part in the main inscription. The surface of the architrave, but not the signs themselves, indicates minor repair with pinkish gypsum plaster; and the same material was used to join the two blocks together as well as the 'corner piece' bearing the name of Teti.

(1) *ḥtp dj nswt ḥtp Jnpw qrs.t(j).f m ẖrt-nṯr m zmjt jmntjt j3w nfr wrt wn jm3ḫ.f ḫ[r][12] Ttj m ḥtp m ḥtp ḫr nṯr ꜥ3 m nb jm3ḫ jmj-r st ḫntj-š pr-ꜥ3 Mḥ-n.s njs*[13] *Mḥj* (2) *ḥtp dj nswt Wsjr prt-ḫrw (n)*[14] *.f m wp rnpt Ḏḥwtjt tpj rnpt W3g ḥb Zkr m ḥb hrw nb m 3wt wn jm3ḫ.f ḫr msw.f špsj nswt Mḥ-n.s njs Mḥ[j]* (3) *ḥtp dj nswt ḥtp Jnpw ḥp.f m ḥtp ḥr w3wt nfr(w)t nt jmnt ḥppt jm3ḫw ḥr.sn ḫr nṯrw nbw jmnt m ḥzzw nswt m jr ḥtpt m zb jm3ḫ*[15] *m ḏd m3ꜥt mrrt nṯr*[16] (4) *j ꜥnḫw tpjw t3 jm3ḫw ḫr nṯr sw3.t(j).sn ḥr jz pn st mw prt-ḫrw m ntt m ḫt.tn jr nfr wnn m ḫt.tn ḏd m r.k*[17] *wdn m ꜥw(j).k ḫ3 t p3t ḥnqt ḫ3 šs ḫ3 k3 ḫ3 3pd rnp(w)t nb(t) n jm3ḫw ḫr nṯr* (5) *jnk ḏd nfr wḥm nfr jr m3ꜥt mrrt nṯr jnk jr ḥtp sb jm3ḫ jr rmṯ nb prt-ḫrw jw(.j) r-ḫ3.sn m ẖrt-nṯr m jmnt jnk 3ḫ jqr ḥk3 ꜥpr mrjj rmṯ ḥzw nṯr jm3ḫw ḫr nswt* (6) *jr.n(.j) jz pn ꜥnḫ.k(wj) ḥr rdwj(.j) m ḥzjj n nswt mrjj n rmṯ rdj.n(.j) ḏb3w n ḫrtjw-nṯr r ḥtp.sn ḥr.s wp.n(.j) sn-nw r ḥtp.sn m sḫm(.j)*[18] (7) *jn mrr nswt jm3ḫw ḫr nṯr ꜥ3 qrss.t(j).f nfr m ẖrt-nṯr sw3t.t(j).f ḥr jz pn ḏdt.t(j).f*[19] *t ḥnqt n Mḥ-n.s njsw*[20] *m Mḥj jr n Ḫntj ḏd.tn jnk jz jm3ḫw mj wn ḏdt jr tp t3 jnk wnnt jr ḥtpt sb jm3ḫw.* '(1) An offering which the king gives and an offering which Anubis (gives): that he be buried in the necropolis in the western desert, at a very good old age, and that his honour be before Teti. In peace, in peace before the great god, as a possessor of veneration, the overseer of the department of the *ḫntj-š* officials, Mehnes, called Mehi. (2) An offering which the king gives and Osiris (gives). May an invocation offering come forth (for) him on the opening of the year feast, the Thot-feast, the first of the year feast, the Wag-feast, the Sokar-feast and on the daily feast, in perpetuity, that his honour be before his children, the nobleman of the king, Mehnes, called Mehi. (3) An offering which the king gives and an offering which Anubis (gives), that he may travel in peace upon the beautiful roads of the west, upon which the honoured ones travel before the gods, lords of the west, as one who is favoured of the king, as one who achieved graciousness, as one who attained honour, as one who said the truth which the god loves. (4) O you living people, who are upon earth, who are honoured before the god, and who will pass by this tomb: place water and offerings from that which is in your possession. If there is nothing in your possession, (then) say with your mouth and offer with your hands: A thousand of bread, cake and beer, a thousand of alabaster, a thousand of oxen, a thousand of fowl, all year-offerings for the honoured one before the god. (5) I was one who said what was good, who reported what was good and who did justice which the god loves. I was one who achieved graciousness and who attained honour. As for all persons who invoke offerings (for me), I shall be their backer in the necropolis in the west. I am an excellent spirit, an equipped magician, one who is beloved of the people, favoured of the god and honoured before the king. (6) I made this tomb while I was alive, on my feet, as one favoured of the king and beloved of the people. I made payments to the stone-masons so they were satisfied about it. I judged the two partners so that they were satisfied with my authority. (7) Indeed, one beloved of the king and honoured before the great god, and one who will be buried well in the necropolis, is he who will pass by this tomb and who will say: bread and beer for Mehnes, who is called Mehi, born to Khenti. May you say: I was indeed an honoured one, as being said upon earth. I was indeed one who achieved graciousness and who attained honours'.

The False Door of Mehi

Pls. 7-8.

The Upper Lintel: (1) *ḥtp dj nswt ḥtp dj Jnpw ḫntj zḥ-nṯr qrs.t(j).f m ẖrt-nṯr nfr wrt* (2) *dj jmnt ꜥ.s r.f m jrt ḥtpt sb jm3ḫw smr wꜥtj Mḥj* '(1) An offering which the king gives and an offering which Anubis foremost of the divine booth gives: that he be buried in the necropolis very well.[21] (2) May the West[22] give her arm[23] to him, as one who achieved graciousness and one who attained honour, the sole companion,[24] Mehi'. A standing figure of the owner holding the staff and sceptre is depicted.

The Central Panel: Extending his hand towards an offering table, Mehi sits next to an unnamed woman. Before his face is written: *špsj nswt pr-ꜥ3 sḥḏ ḫntj-š Mḥj* 'the king's nobleman of the palace, the superintendent of the *ḫntj-š* officials, Mehi'. Below the table are a ewer and a text: *k3 3pd ḫ3 t ḥnqt ḫ3* 'oxen, fowl, one thousand, bread, beer, one thousand'.

The Lower Lintel: (1) *ḥtp dj nswt dj Wsjr ḫntj Ḏdw ḥp.f nfr ḥr w3wt nfr(w)t ḫppt jm3ḫw ḥr.sn* (2) *šms.t(j).f ḥr w3wt ḏsr(w)t šmst jm3ḫw ḥr-sn špsj nswt Mḥj* '(1) An offering which the king gives and which Osiris foremost of Busiris gives, that he may travel well upon the beautiful roads, upon which the honoured ones travel, (2) that he may be accompanied upon the sacred roads, upon which the honoured ones are accompanied, the nobleman of the king, Mehi'.

The Right Outer Jamb: (1) *ḥtp dj nswt ḥtp dj Jnpw ḫntj zḥ-nṯr qrs.f*[25] *m ḫrt-nṯr šsp nṯr ᶜ.f r*[26] *swt wᶜb(w)t* (2) *ḥtp dj nswt Wsjr ḥp.f nfr ḥr w3wt jptf ḫppt jm3ḫw ḥr.sn* (3) *ḥtp dj nswt šms.t(j).f ḥr w3wt ḏsr(w)t šmst jm3ḫw ḥr.sn jᶜ.f n nṯr ᶜ3* '(1) An offering which the king gives and an offering which Anubis foremost of the divine booth gives. May he be buried in the necropolis, may the god receive his arm at the pure places. (2) An offering which the king gives and Osiris (gives), that he may travel well upon those roads, upon which the honoured ones travel. (3) An offering which the king gives, that he may be accompanied upon the sacred roads, upon which the honoured ones are accompanied, that he may ascend to the great god'. Each of the three vertical columns of text ends in a representation of the owner standing, holding his staff.

The Right Inner Jamb: *jmj-r ḫntj-š špsj nswt sḥḏ ḫntj-š jm3ḫw ḫr Wsjr ḫr nṯr ᶜ3*[27] *Mḥj* 'the overseer of the *ḫntj-š* officials, the nobleman of the king, the superintendent of the *ḫntj-š* officials, the honoured one before Osiris and before the great god, Mehi'. A standing figure of the owner with his staff is depicted at the bottom of the jamb.[28]

The left outer and inner jambs are identical with the right ones.

The False Door of Khenti

Pl. 9.

The Upper Lintel: *ḥtp dj nswt Jnpw tpj ḏw.f jm3ḫwt* 'An offering which the king gives and Anubis who is on his hill (gives). The honoured one'.

The Right Outer Jamb: *jm3ḫwt ḫr Ptḥ Ḫntj* 'the honoured one before Ptah, Khenti'. The owner is shown smelling a lotus flower.

The Left Outer Jamb: *rḫt nswt jm3ḫwt Ṯtj* 'the acquaintance of the king, the honoured one, Tjeti'. A figure of the owner smelling a lotus flower is depicted.

The Central Panel: The owner sits at an offering table. Before her face is written: *ḫ3 t ḥnqt k3 3pd* 'a thousand of bread, beer, oxen and fowl'. On the other side of the table food and drink are represented.

The Lower Lintel: *jm3ḫwt Ṯtj* 'the honoured one, Tjeti'.

The Right Inner Jamb: *jm3hwt Ṯtj* 'the honoured one, Tjeti'.

The Left Inner Jamb: *jm3ḫwt Ḫntj* 'the honoured one, Khenti'.

NOTES

1. Ranke, *Personennamen* 1, 163:23.
2. The name is not attested in ibid.
3. Ibid, 271:19.
4. Ibid, 395:5.
5. For a discussion of this date see Kanawati, *GM* 83 [1984], 33-35.
6. Our thanks are due to Dr. Mahmud Abd El-Razik for permission to use information from his excavations. See also ibid, 33-34; *Saqqara* 1, 9.
7. Goedicke, *Königliche Dokumente*, 37-38, fig. 3; Kanawati, *GM* 83 [1984], 33.
8. *Saqqara* 1, pl. 29. Notice that this phonetic writing is not used on the adjacent wall (ibid, pl. 30).
9. Schenkel, *Frühmittelägyptische*, 40, 107.

10. Firth-Gunn, *Teti Pyr. Cem.* 2, pls. 58, 60; Jéquier, *Particuliers,* passim.
11. Firth-Gunn, *Teti Pyr. Cem.* 2, pl. 70:1; Dunham, *Naga-Ed-Dêr,* passim.
12. This seems a better reading than the *wn jm3ḫw ḫft Ttj* (*GM* 83 [1984], 31-33). The same form is used in line 2: *wn jm3ḫ.f ḫr msw.f.*
13. For the use of *njs* 'called' to introduce a second name in the Old Kingdom cf. *Wb.* 2, 204:16.
14. The *n* is missing.
15. For similar expressions see Junker, *Gîza* 7, 208ff; Fischer, *Metropolitan* 1, 167ff.
16. The determinative after *nṯr* is certainly the falcon on the stand (Gardiner, *Grammar,* G7), as in *jr m3ʿt mrrt nṯr* (line 5) and in *jm3ḫw ḫr nṯr* (line 4). The other instances of the word *nṯr* are followed by the seated god (ibid, A40).
17. After addressing the living in plural and using the suffix *ṯn,* the scribe reverts to the singular in *r.k* and *ʿwj.k.*
18. Alternatively, it could be *m sḫmt.n.j jm* 'in so far as I was able/in that over which I had control' (James, *Khentika,* 40-41, pl. 6; see also Sethe, *Urk.*1, 199:2, 200:17).
19. The last three phrases use the usual *sḏm.tj.fj* form, but in addition it appears that with the verb *qrs,* the *sḏmm.f* form was employed (Gardiner, *Grammar* §425-26) and with the verbs *sw3* and *ḏd* the *sḏmt.f* form was used (ibid §406).
20. This is probably a participle of the verb *njs.*
21. It is possible that the word *j3w* was omitted here.
22. On the personification of the west see, for example, Davies et al, *Saqqâra Tombs* 1, fig. 2; Saqqara 1, 18.
23. That is, her assistance.
24. This title begins in line 1 and continues in line 2. It should possibly precede the name.
25. The usual *sḏm.t(j).f* form is not used here, nor in the following phrase, *šsp nṯr ʿ.f.*
26. The *r* is missing on the opposite jamb.
27. *ʿ3* is omitted on the opposite jamb.
28. It is doubtful whether the figure on the opposite jamb also holds a sceptre.

THE MASTABA OF HESI

I THE TOMB OWNER AND HIS FAMILY

The Tomb Owner

NAME

Ḥzjj[1] 'Hesi'.

TITLES

1 – *jmj-r jmjt ṯnwj* 'overseer of that which is within the boundaries (of the cultivation)'.[2] This unusual title could be an extension of other titles frequently held by officials buried in this cemetery as, for example, 'overseer of all that heaven gives and earth produces', 'overseer of the marshlands', 'overseer of the two fields of offerings', etc.
2 – *jmj-r Šmꜥ* 'overseer of Upper Egypt'.[3]
3 – *ḫrp šnḏt nbt* 'director of every kilt'.[4]
4 – *ẖrj-ḥbt* 'lector priest'.
5 – *sm* 'sem-priest'.[5]
6 – *smr wꜥtj* 'sole companion'.
7 – *sḏ3wtj-bjtj* 'treasurer of the king of Lower Egypt'.

A Relative(?) of Hesi

NAME

Ttj-ꜥnḫ[6] 'Tetiankh'. Although a separate room, in which a false door was placed, is assigned to Tetiankh, no relationship to Hesi is recorded.

TITLES

1 – *ẖrj-ḥbt* 'lector-priest'.
2 – *smr wꜥtj* 'sole companion'.

II DATING OF HESI

(1) The mastaba of Hesi is adjacent to that of Mehi, their façades having been constructed as one wall, with no indication that one mastaba was built against the other. Furthermore, the recess of Mehi's façade extends westward beyond the line of the west wall of his chapel. This could only occur if Hesi's façade, the east wall of his chapel and the filling core between this and Mehi's mastaba were built simultaneously with the last.

(2) The plan of the chapel, with multiple interior rooms and the use of deep shafts leading to the burial chambers, resembles the great mastabas of officials in the period from Teti-early Pepy I[7] rather than those of Pepy II.[8] Late in Pepy I's reign even the viziers Rawer[9] and Tjetju[10] built chapels of only one room; and one would not expect an overseer of Upper Egypt from Pepy II's reign to be buried in the Teti cemetery.

(3) The false door of Hesi accords stylistically with others from the time of Pepy I,[11] and its very elongated panel is characteristic of this reign.[12]

(4) The absence of the ranking titles *jrj-pꜥt* or *ḥ3tj-ꜥ* for an overseer of Upper Egypt is noteworthy. The same phenomenon is observable in the case of Khui, another overseer of Upper Egypt buried close by;[13] of the vizier Idu/Nfr, buried at Giza;[14] and of Nekhebu, also buried at Giza,[15] who was 'overseer of all the works of the king'. All these men date to Pepy I's reign.

(5) The expression *jmjt ṯnwj,* in the title *jmj-r jmjt ṯnwj,* is uncommon, but is found in a number of tombs dating from the reigns of Teti and Pepy I.[16]

(6) The reference to being honoured before Herishef (Arsaphes)[17] might indicate that Hesi originated from Heracleopolis or that he spent a period of employment there. It should not point to the Heracleopolitan period, for neither the style of the false door, nor the use of the determinative ⊗ in the epithet *jmj wt* of Anubis,[18] would support such a date.

Three overseers of Upper Egypt are buried to the north of the mastabas of Mereruka and Kagemni. These are Nikauisesi from the reign of Teti,[19] and Hesi and Khui from that of Pepy I. Hesi is probably to be dated, like his neighbour Mehi, to the beginning of Pepy I's reign, while Khui must be a little later.[20] Nikauisesi, Hesi and Khui appear to have followed each other as overseers of Upper Egypt, but not necessarily as immediate successors.

Suggested date: Early Pepy I.

III ARCHITECTURAL FEATURES

Pl. 10.

The mastaba of Hesi is situated to the north of Tjetji and to the west of Mehi, with its entrance in the south wall facing the third street behind Mereruka. The tomb is composed of five chambers and nine shafts. Well preserved mud brick walls with an average height of 2.00m. show traces of black mud plaster throughout. The floors of all chambers are coated with mud plaster with an average thickness of .12m.

The mastaba is rectangular in shape measuring 7.70m. N-S and 9.40m. E-W. This last measurement is not final as the western perimeter wall was only exposed to a thickness of .30m. when excavation work ceased. The north, south and east walls are of an almost uniform thickness of .75m.-.80m. Where the east wall lies parallel to the mastaba of Mehi, its thickness is .40m. with the remaining .40m. to the west wall of Mehi being filled with a core of compacted rubble, sand and earth.

The tomb is entered through a doorway, .60m. wide, positioned in the eastern half of the south wall and set within a recess .12m. deep and 2.00m. long. The entrance opens to Room A which measures 3.10m. E-W, 1.90m. N-S along the east wall and 1.60m. N-S along the west wall. The variation in the length of these two walls is caused by the construction of the north wall which is not parallel to the south wall. Shaft I, with a mouth .90m. square, is found immediately to the west of the entrance doorway. Shafts IV and VIII were completely excavated but the other shafts in this mastaba were cleared only to base rock level. The position and size of their mouths can be provided but no further measurements.

Although the ceiling of Room A has been destroyed, a few centimetres of the spring of an arch, visible at the top of the north and south walls, indicate that it would have been covered with a vaulted roof. Two doorways in the east and west walls, both .60m. wide and located .15m. from the south wall, provide the entrances from this chamber to Room B and Room E.

Room B is a long, corridor-like chamber, measuring 4.10m. N-S x 1.00m. E-W, and like Room A shows remnants of the spring of a vaulted ceiling, here found on the east and west walls.

At the northern end of Room B are the entrances to two rooms, Room C to the west and Room D to the north. A doorway .50m. wide, located .35m. from the north wall of Room B gives access to Room C. It measures 3.10m. E-W, 1.90m. N-S at the west wall and 1.60m. N-S at the east wall. The limestone false door of Hesi was found in this room having fallen from a recess in the west wall .70m. wide and .25m. deep. The false door was broken into two pieces with a total height of 1.38m. and width of .65m. A plastered, mud brick platform before the false door measures 1.90m. long x .50m. deep x .12m. high. In the south-east corner of Room C is the opening to Shaft IX. The mouth of this shaft is 2.00m. square and the angled north wall of Room A passes across the southern part of the mouth.

Separated from Room C by an internal wall .65m. thick is the long, narrow Room D measuring 1.30m. N-S x 4.70m. E-W. The perimeter walls of the mastaba form the north and east walls of this room while the west wall is almost entirely occupied by the limestone false door of Tetiankh. The upper section of this false door is missing, but the lower portion, measuring .90m. x .90m., was discovered *in situ* above a mud platform, 1.30m. long, .17m. deep and .07m. high. The brick wall at both sides of the false door retains remnants of white plaster.

A narrow, rectangular shaft, Shaft VIII, measuring 2.30m. N-S x .90m. E-W, is located 1.60m. east of the false door, its southern edge being formed by the south wall of Room D. Two other shafts, possibly part of a mastaba to the north, are also cut into the perimeter wall of Hesi. Both have mouths 1.00m. square, with the first lying .35m. to the east of Shaft IX and .35m. to the north of Room D. This shaft has an upper section of mud brick 2.10m. high and descends through the bedrock for 2.00m. It has no burial chamber. The second shaft is built .20m. further to the east, intruding slightly on the north wall of Hesi.

Rooms A to D are all situated in the eastern part of the mastaba and are separated from Room E in the western section by a wall .55m. thick lying perpendicular to the façade wall. The room, which measures 4.80m. N-S, 3.00m. E-W on the south wall and 2.80m. E-W on the north wall, is entered through a doorway .60m. wide in the west wall of Room A.

Six shafts were found within Room E. Shafts II and III were dug into the SE and SW corners respectively, while Shafts VI and VII are sited in the NW and NE corners. Shaft IV, which had only been cut through the rock to a depth of .75m., lies against the east wall, .50m. to the north of Shaft II, while Shaft V is placed .70m. north of Shaft III along the west wall. The measurements of the mouths are very similar, being 1.00m. square (Shaft II), 1.20m. square (Shafts III, VI, VII) and 1.10m. E-W x 1.20m. N-S (Shafts (IV and V). Shaft III has a step .50m. wide, 1.20m. long and .15m. deep cut in the rock in the northern side.

IV BURIAL APARTMENTS

Pl. 10.

The mastaba contains nine shafts, but only two of these, IV and VIII, were cleared.

SHAFT IV

This shaft is cut into the rock floor of Room E. It measures 1.10m. E-W x 1.20m. N-S x .75m. deep and has no burial chamber.

SHAFT VIII

The shaft measures 2.30m. N-S x .90m. E-W. It has an upper section of mud brick to a height of 1.60m. and a lower, rock-cut section of 2.60m. It has no burial chamber. The date of Shaft VIII is uncertain but it was undoubtedly added after the original construction was completed as it cuts through the northern perimeter wall. A brick wall, .40m. thick and 1.60m. high on the eastern side of the shaft, supports this assumption since it does not link structurally with either the north or the south walls of Room D. A similar wall may have been built on the western side of the shaft but no trace now remains.

V SCENES AND INSCRIPTIONS

The False Door of Hesi

Pls. 11-12.

The scene and inscriptions on the panel are in very shallow bas relief while those on other parts of the door are incised. Each of the lintels and outer jambs have two lines of inscriptions ending in a standing figure of the owner holding a staff and sceptre. The inner jambs bear the same number of lines, but end with a small representation of Hesi, holding a long staff while seated.

The Upper Lintel: (1) *ḥtp dj nswt ḥtp Jnpw tpj ḏw.f n smr wꜥtj Ḥzjj* (2) *ḥtp dj nswt Wsjr n smr wꜥtj ẖrj-ḥbt* '(1) An offering which the king gives and an offering which Anubis who is on his hill (gives) to the sole companion, Hesi. (2) An offering which the king gives and Osiris (gives) to the sole companion, the lector priest'.

The Central Panel: Hesi sits on a chair with a low back and lion's legs. He wears a shoulder-length wig and places his left hand on his chest, while his right is extended towards an offering table laden with twelve loaves of bread. Below the table are a stand with some jars and a ewer. A line of inscriptions runs across the top of the panel and continues above the head of the owner: *sḏ3wtj-bjtj jmj-r*

Šmʿ smr wʿtj Ḥzjj 'the treasurer of the king of Lower Egypt, the overseer of Upper Egypt, the sole companion, Hesi'. Above the table is written: (1) *ḫ3 t ḫ3 ḥnqt ḫ3 p3t* (2) *ḫ3 k3 ḫ3 3pd ḫ3 šs mnḫt* '(1) one thousand of bread, one thousand of beer, one thousand of cake, (2) one thousand of oxen, one thousand of fowl, one thousand of alabaster and clothes'.

The Lower Lintel: (1) *smr wʿtj ẖrj-ḥbt Ḥzjj* (2) *jm3ḫw ḫr nb.f* '(1) the sole companion, the lector priest, Hesi, (2) the honoured one before his lord'.

The Right Outer Jamb: (1) *smr wʿtj ẖrj-ḥbt jm3ḫw ḫr Ptḥ-rsj-jnb.f ḫr Wsjr Ḥzjj* (2) *smr wʿtj ẖrj-ḥbt jm3ḫw ḫr Ḥrj-š.f ḫr Jnpw tpj ḏw.f nb t3 ḏsr* '(1) the sole companion, the lector priest, the honoured one before Ptah south of his wall[21] and before Osiris, Hesi, (2) the sole companion, the lector priest, the honoured one before Herishef (Arsaphes) and before Anubis who is on his hill, lord of the sacred land'.

The Left Outer Jamb: (1) *smr wʿtj ẖrj-ḥbt jm3ḫw ḫr Jnpw tpj ḏw.f ḫntj zḥ-nṯr jmj wt Ḥzjj* (2) *smr wʿtj ẖrj-ḥbt jm3ḫw ḫr Ḥrj-š.f ḫr Wsjr nb Ḏdw* '(1) the sole companion, the lector priest, the honoured one before Anubis who is on his hill, foremost of the divine booth, who is in the embalming place, Hesi, (2) the sole companion, the lector priest, the honoured one before Herishef (Arsaphes) and before Osiris lord of Busiris'.

The Right Inner Jamb: (1) *sm ḫrp šndt nbt smr wʿtj jm3ḫw Ḥzjj* (2) *smr wʿtj ẖrj-ḥbt jm3ḫw mrr nb.f* '(1) the sem-priest, the director of every kilt, the sole companion, the honoured one, Hesi, (2) the sole companion, the lector priest, the honoured one, the beloved of his lord'.

The Left Inner Jamb: (1) *smr wʿtj ẖrj-ḥbt jmj-r jmjt ṯnwj Ḥzjj* (2) *smr wʿtj ẖrj-ḥbt jm3ḫw ḫr nṯr ʿ3* '(1) the sole companion, the lector priest, the overseer of that which is within the boundaries (of the cultivation), Hesi, (2) the sole companion, the lector priest, the honoured one before the great god'.

The False Door of Tetiankh

Pl. 13.

All the decoration on this door is incised. Each of the jambs has two columns of text, ending in one or more horizontal lines giving the titles and name of the owner and followed by his standing figure holding the staff and sceptre. The upper part of the door is missing.

The Lower Lintel: *smr wʿtj ẖrj-ḥbt Ttj-ʿnḫ* 'the sole companion, the lector priest, Tetiankh'.

The Right Outer Jamb: (1) . . . *Jnpw tpj ḏw.f jmj wt nb t3 ḏsr n smr wʿtj ẖrj-ḥbt Ttj-ʿnḫ* (2) . . . *[jm3ḫ]w ḫr Wsjr nb 3bḏw* '(1) . . . Anubis who is on his hill, who is in the embalming place, lord of the sacred land, for the sole companion, the lector priest, Tetiankh. (2) . . . the honoured one before Osiris lord of Abydos'.

The Right Inner Jamb: (1) *ḥtp dj nswt Wsjr n smr wʿtj Ttj-ʿnḫ* (2) *prt-ḫrw n.f m ẖrt-nṯr zmjt jmntjt* '(1) An offering which the king gives and Osiris (gives) for the sole companion, Tetiankh. (2) May an invocation offering come forth for him in the necropolis of the western desert'.

The two left jambs are identical with the right ones.

NOTES

1. Ranke, *Personennamen* 1, 254:29.
2. For the reading and significance of *jmjt ṯnwj* see Firth-Gunn, *Teti Pyr. Cem.* 1, 155; James, *Khentika*, 49.
3. For a study of this office see Martin-Pardey, *Provinzialverwaltung*, 152ff.
4. Helck, *Beamtentitel*, 18, 35.
5. Ibid.
6. Ranke, *Personennamen* 1, 384:15.
7. For example, Duell, *Mereruka*, pl. 1; Badawy, *Nyhetep-Ptah*, fig. 17; James, *Khentika*, pl. 3; Davies et al., *Saqqâra Tombs* 1, pls. 1, 19-20; Nikauisesi (unpublished).
8. Jéquier, *Particuliers*, passim; Jéquier, *Monument funéraire* 3, 50ff.

9. El-Fikey, *Rē-wer,* fig. 2.
10. Firth-Gunn, *Teti Pyr. Cem.* 2, pl. 51.
11. See, for example, that of the firmly-dated official Weni (Fischer, *Varia,* pl. 20).
12. Strudwick, *Administration,* 18; James, *Khentika,* pls. 18-19; Abder-Raziq, in *Mélanges Mokhtar* 2, pl. 1; Junker, *Gîza* 8, figs. 32, 34.
13. Drioton, *ASAE* 43 [1943], 502-504.
14. Junker, *Gîza* 8, 69ff. For dating see Kanawati, *Governmental Reforms,* 35.
15. Strudwick, *Administration,* 113.
16. For example, Kagemni (von Bissing, *Gem-ni-kai* 2, pl. 5); Khentika (James, *Khentika,* pl. 14); Tjetju (Firth-Gunn, *Teti Pyr. Cem.* 1, 155).
17. *L.Ä.* II, 1015ff; Fischer, *Metropolitan* 1, 161, 29 add.; Gomaà, *Zwischenzeit,* 133.
18. Schenkel, *Frühmittelägyptische,* 40, 107.
19. He is mentioned in a royal decree issued by Teti (Goedicke, *Königliche Dokumente,* fig. 3).
20. Kanawati, *Governmental Reforms,* 31ff.; *Saqqara* 1, 12; Kanawati, *Chron.d'Ég.* 56 [1981], 210ff.
21. For some examples see Firth-Gunn, *Teti Pyr. Cem.* 1, 222, 226; Hassan, *Saqqara* 3, 16; Alliot, *Tell Edfou* 1933, 24, 25; Sethe, *Urk.* 1, 251:18, 252:4.

MASTABA C

I ARCHITECTURAL FEATURES

Pl. 14.

Mastaba C lies immediately to the north of the tomb of Iri/Tetiseneb and to the east of that of Ishfi, with its entrance facing north to the fourth street behind Mereruka.

It is rectangular in shape, measuring 4.65m. N-S x 3.80m. E-W (minimum). This last measurement is incomplete as the east wall, extending beyond the boundary of the concession as in the case of the mastaba of Iri/Tetiseneb, was not fully excavated. Mastaba C contains a chapel and five shafts with the extant walls preserved to a height of 1.80m. above rock level. The original chapel may have been a single room extending the full length of the mastaba similar to other tombs in this area with N-S chapels (Ihyemsaf, Iries, Irenakhti, Tjetji, Tjetetu, Mehi and Ishfi), with Shafts IV and V being later additions. A wall constructed across the width of the chapel and 2.05m. from the entrance, supplies evidence for the reuse of the tomb. This wall, measuring 1.50m. E-W with a thickness of .40m., is formed of a mixture of mud bricks and stones different to the other walls of the mastaba and similar to materials used in the construction of Shaft III in the mastaba of Ishfi (see under Ishfi). It does not link with the east and west walls and while its southern face, which forms the upper part of Shaft IV, is smooth, the northern face, visible from the chapel, was left rough with projecting boulders. Further evidence for the reuse of the tomb is the absence of a lintel and the deliberate blocking of the entrance doorway with compacted debris upon which a wall was built. Such a construction indicates that the chapel had been filled and that this wall was built above what appeared at that time to be firm ground.

The entrance to the chapel is in the western half of the north wall of the mastaba with the door centrally placed in a recess measuring 2.05m. long x .15m. deep. The doorway is .65m. wide x .40m. deep and is sited slightly to the east of the central axis of the chapel. No lintel was found.

The chapel as it stands now measures 2.05m. N-S and 1.50m. E-W. The west wall is formed by the east wall of the mastaba of Ishfi and contains a recess 1.60m. high x .80m. wide x .30m. deep, positioned .80m. from the entrance wall. This recess is lined with brick and coated with mud plaster. Mud plaster also covers the base of the recess to a depth of .15m. A small, square shaft (V) is situated against the east wall of the chapel with the later, transverse brick and rubble wall rising above its southern edge. A large shaft (IV) occupies the remaining area of the chapel from this intrusive wall to the southern limit of the mastaba.

II BURIAL APARTMENTS

Pl. 14.

The mastaba contains five shafts, three of which are found to the east of the chapel, while two lie within the chapel area. All were found plundered.

SHAFT I

The main shaft has a mouth 1.50m. square and is situated in the NE corner of the mastaba. All of its walls are lined with mud brick, with the west wall formed by the east wall of the chapel and the north wall by the façade wall. The brickwork is preserved to a height of 2.60m. above rock level, the larger part of the shaft having been cut through the bedrock to a depth of 5.80m. At the base of the shaft an opening 1.30m. high in the west wall gives access to a rectangular chamber measuring 3.80m. N-S x 2.10m. E-W, with a height of 1.65m. The floor level of this burial chamber is .35m. below that of the shaft. Within the chamber a burial pit, measuring 1.90m. N-S x .70m. E-W, has been cut into the bedrock. It is surrounded by a ledge .20m. high and .30m. wide on the north, east and west, and .45m. on the south side. The burial pit is not positioned in the centre of the chamber, but closer to the shaft. A stone lid 2.30m. in length, 1.00m. in width and .35m. deep was found broken into two pieces. The southern portion was still *in situ,* but the northern section was on the floor of the chamber.

SHAFT II

This shaft lies .50m. south of Shaft I with its east wall aligned with that of the main shaft and .85m. from the east wall of Shaft IV. It has a mouth 1.20m. square and descends to a depth of 4.30m. An upper section of mud brick is now irregular in height with an average measurement of 1.30m., while the rock cut lower portion continues to an average depth of 3.00m. At the base of the shaft and in its west wall is a burial chamber measuring 2.06m. N-S x 1.40m. E-W, with a height of .80m.

SHAFT III

This smaller shaft is positioned .25m. south of Shaft II and .95m. east of Shaft IV. It is cut over the southern perimeter of Mastaba C and into the northern part of the mastaba of Iri/Tetiseneb. Its west wall is aligned with that of Shaft II of Iri/Tetiseneb. It has a mouth .95m. square and descends to a depth of 2.30m., of which 1.90m. has been cut through the bedrock. No burial chamber was found.

SHAFT IV

Shaft IV is cut into the southern part of the chapel and measures 1.65m. N-S x 1.50m. E-W, with a depth of 3.40m. The upper section of the shaft has an average height of 2.10m. and was built of mud brick on the eastern, western and southern sides, while the northern side was formed by a wall of stone and brick extending across the full width of the chapel. Below the brick lined portion, the shaft continues down through rock for a further 1.30m. No burial chamber was found.

SHAFT V

The northern face of the rock and brick wall which divides the chapel forms the southern border of this unfinished shaft. Its eastern side lies along the east wall of the chapel while the northern and western sides are defined by a rock ledge, .10m. high and .15m. wide. The mouth of the shaft is .80m. square and the depth through the bedrock is .70m. from the ledge to the floor of the shaft.

THE MASTABA OF ISHFI/ISHFU

I THE TOMB OWNER

NAMES

1 – *Jšfw*[1] 'Ishfu'. This name is now visible only on the entrance lintel.
2 – *Jšfj*[2] 'Ishfi'. This name, which has been inscribed a number of times on the false door, has been chiselled out in every case. However, the remaining parts of the signs make the reading of the name possible.

TITLES

1 – *jmj-r st ḫntj-š pr-ˁ3* 'overseer of the department of the *ḫntj-š* officials of the palace'.
2 – *jrj-pˁt* 'hereditary prince'.
3 – *ḥ3tj-ˁ* 'count'.
4 – *ḥrj-sšt3* 'privy to the secret'.
5 – *smr wˁtj* 'sole companion'.
6 – *sḥḏ ḫntj-š pr-ˁ3* 'superintendent of the *ḫntj-š* officials of the palace'.
7 – *špsj nswt* 'nobleman of the king'.

II DATING AND IDENTITY OF ISHFI

The false door and the entrance lintel of Ishfi/Ishfu were found in the burial chamber of shaft I of the mastaba. Although broken into five pieces, all parts of the false door were present, which suggests that it was 'thrown' down into the shaft when this was still empty, and was perhaps even pushed into the burial chamber. Inscribed stone objects, large and small, seem to have been left *in situ* in this section of the cemetery, and it is therefore unlikely that such a heavy false door would be transported for any distance simply to be dumped into this shaft. The south end of a niche built in the brick of the west wall of the chapel is clear, and the space to the north of this allows for a door of this size. It seems most likely that the false door and the lintel were removed during the reuse of the tomb (see below).

The tomb of Ishfi is built against the mastabas of Mehi and Hesi and uses parts of their walls as common walls. Ishfi must therefore have been later than the other two officials, but not necessarily by much. The type of his false door and the palaeographic details point to a date in the middle of Dynasty 6.

The erasure of his name and figure may be linked with the similar phenomenon observed in the tombs of a number of individuals in charge of the *ḫntj-š* officials.[3] This may also be connected with the somewhat unsettled period of Pepy I's reign, when his wife was brought to trial and when Weni replaced four *jmjw-r ḫntj-š pr-ˁ3*, with the explanation that his responsibility was to provide protection for the king.[4]

It is surprising to find the ranks of *jrj-pˁt* and *ḥ3tj-ˁ* held by a man with Ishfi's responsibilities. There is no reason to believe that such ranks were usurped at the time, and it is more likely that Ishfi 'inherited'(?) them from his father. This would presuppose that the latter was one of the higher officials, or even a vizier, under Teti or early in Pepy I's reign. The name Ishfi is unattested, as far as we know, except in the mastaba of the vizier Ankhmahor, in the near vicinity in the Teti cemetery.[5] It may be argued that our Ishfi was not Ankhmahor's son, since the latter added a room in his father's chapel: his false door still stands.[6] On the other hand, an analysis of the family representations in Ankhmahor's chapel suggests the existence of two sons, both described as eldest,[7] with the name of Ishfi.[8] These two sons are represented in the same scene,[9] one shown before Ankhmahor's leg, with the designation *smr wˁtj ẖrj-ḥbt Jšfj* 'the sole companion, the lector priest, Ishfi', while the other is depicted as an offering bearer, labelled *z3.f smsw n ẖt.f mrjj.f sḥḏ ḫntj-š pr-ˁ3 Jšfj* 'his eldest son of his body, his beloved, the superintendent of the *ḫntj-š* officials of the palace, Ishfi'.[10] That the first Ishfi was also an eldest son is indicated by his representation behind his father with the designation *z3.f n ẖt.f smsw smr wˁtj Jšfj* 'his eldest son of his body, the sole companion, Ishfi'.[11]

It is reasonable to think that the son described as *smr wꜥtj ẖrj-ḥbt* and represented immediately before Ănkhmahor is his real eldest son, who later added a false door in his father's chapel, with the names of *Jšfj* and *Twtw*.[12] In his long list of titles *Jšfj/Twtw* does not show a connection with the *ḫntj-š* officials, as does his brother the *sḥḏ ḫntj-š pr-ꜥ3*, who was probably our Ishfi. The latter was probably an eldest son of Ankhmahor, but by a second marriage. It is curious that the truly eldest son, owner of the false door in Ankhmahor's chapel, and holder of very high administrative offices[13] (excluding that of vizier), did not record the ranks of *jrj-pꜥt* and *ḥ3tj-ꜥ*, while the second Ishfi, a mere *jmj-r st ḫntj-š pr-ꜥ3*, was elevated to such ranks. The case highlights the uncertainty surrounding the problem of the transmission of honorific titles. It is unlikely that the choice of which of his sons would succeed to his titles lay with Ankhmahor. That the first Ishfi was his preferred choice (because he was truly the 'eldest' son) may be inferred from the fact that a room was allocated to him in his father's tomb. But it remains possible that the second Ishfi inherited the honours through his mother. Alternatively, we have seen that often high officials who may be dated from the early part of Pepy I's reign, also lack these honorific titles.[14] It may be speculated whether a change in policy during this reign caused the eldest son of a vizier to be excepted from automatic elevation to a comparable status, with the honour being bestowed instead on the second son.

Suggested date: Middle of Pepy I's reign.

III ARCHITECTURAL FEATURES

Pls. 15-16.

This mastaba lies to the north of Mehi and to the west of Mastaba C. It is rectangular in shape, measuring 4.65m. N-S x 5.25m. E-W, and has its entrance in the north wall, opening to the fourth street behind Mereruka like Mastaba C.

The original mastaba was composed of a long N-S chapel in the western part with two square shafts containing burial chambers to its east. A lintel, broken into two pieces totalling .48m. long x .10m. high x .14m. thick, and a large false door, broken into five pieces with a total measurement of 1.55m. x .96m., were found in the burial chamber of Shaft I. Between the two shafts lies a narrow rectangular compartment measuring .70m. N-S x 1.50m. E-W with a depth of 1.80m. The exact purpose of this compartment is unclear but similar areas within the core of the mastaba occur in other tombs nearby.[15]

The chapel is entered through a doorway .60m. wide and .45m. deep which is positioned at the eastern side of the entrance wall. The doorway is set within an entrance recess, .15m. deep, of which only the eastern end measuring .70m. in length is preserved. No measurements can be provided for the western part of the recess, destroyed in the building of a later shaft (Shaft III). However, as the usual practice in nearby tombs was to centrally position the door within the recess, it may be presumed that the western section extended to the same length, .70m., as the eastern side.

The north wall of Mehi's mastaba forms the south wall of Ishfi's chapel while the east wall of Room D of Hesi was used as the southern section of the west wall. Only a small part of the northern section of the west wall is preserved (measuring 1.15m. long x .60m. wide), as the NW corner of the chapel was demolished in the construction of a later shaft (Shaft III). This left only a section .15m. in length of the original entrance wall west of the doorway. The existing height of most walls is approximately 1.90m. and all are coated with black mud plaster.

A platform measuring .80m. in length and .30m. in height is located in the west wall 1.10m. from the southern perimeter of the chapel. A small niche, .30m. wide x .80m. high x .10m. deep, was cut into the west wall south of the platform, while another, larger niche, .65m. wide x .90m. high x .15m. deep, was found immediately to the north of the platform. All were coated with black mud plaster.

IV BURIAL APARTMENTS

Pls. 15-16.

To the east of the chapel two shafts are aligned N-S in the brick core of the mastaba with a later, third shaft built at the NW corner of the tomb. All were found plundered although the broken false door and lintel of Ishfi were found in Shaft I and the false door and one side slab of Mesi were discovered above Shaft III.

SHAFT I

This almost square shaft, measuring 1.55m. N-S x 1.60m. E-W, lies .55m. from the north and east walls of the mastaba and the same distance from the east wall of the chapel. It descends vertically to a depth of 9.70m., having an upper section of mud brick with an extant average height of 1.90m. and a lower rock cut section measuring 7.80m. The shaft narrows to 1.30m. square at the floor where an opening 2.00m. high in the west wall gives access to a burial chamber, 3.40m. in length, N-S. It measures 2.40m. E-W on the north wall and 2.20m. on the south wall. The ceiling slopes from a height of 2.00m. at the entrance of the chamber to 1.70m. at the western wall.

Within the chamber a burial pit 2.35m. N-S x .70m. E-W x .75m. deep is cut into the floor. The pit was covered with a stone slab, measuring 2.55m. N-S, 1.10m. E-W and with a thickness of .20m., which was found broken in half.

In the north wall at the floor of the shaft is a small chamber(?) which possibly served as a store room. This measures .70m. high x .70m. N-S x .85m. E-W.

SHAFT II

Shaft II is aligned N-S with Shaft I and is .55m. from the eastern perimeter wall and 1.10m. from the east wall of the chapel. The external north wall of the mastaba of Mehi forms the south wall of this shaft which has a mouth 1.00m. square and descends to a depth of 6.10m. The upper portion of mud brick has an average height of 1.60m. while the lower rock cut section measures 4.50m. At the floor of the shaft a burial chamber opens into the west wall. This room has a ceiling height of .80m. and an average width of 1.35m. It measures 2.00m. N-S on the west wall but is slightly longer on the east side. A ledge, with an average height of .30m. and a width of .40m., is left in the rock at the base of the walls.

SHAFT III

This rectangular shaft is situated at the NW corner of Ishfi's chapel, extending northward beyond the entrance wall of the tomb for 1.10m. It was made by cutting through the north and part of the west walls of the chapel and erecting an upper section with an average height of 1.70m. and a wall thickness of .30m. This upper part is constructed of mud brick and stones, similar to the E-W wall in the chapel of Mastaba C. The lower section was cut vertically through the bedrock to a depth of 3.80m. where it opens in the east wall at the floor to a burial chamber.

The mouth of the shaft measures 2.20m. N-S x 1.00m. E-W and as it descends through the rock the shaft tapers inward to a measurement of 2.10m. N-S x .90m. E-W. The burial chamber is irregular in shape with its north wall measuring 1.25m. and its south wall .90m. This results in an angled east wall which has a length of 2.20m. The ceiling of the chamber is .90m. high at the western side and rises slightly to 1.00m. at the eastern wall.

Above the mud and stone upper section of the shaft was a portion of another mud brick wall, measuring 2.80m. N-S x 1.25m. E-W with an average height of .90m. The wall had a core of stones and rubble. In front of this wall the false door and side panel of Mesi were found, having fallen from their original location, probably in the wall.

V SCENES AND INSCRIPTIONS

The Entrance Lintel

Pl. 17.

This was found in two pieces in the main shaft, and is inscribed in incised relief: *jrj-[p]ᶜt sḥḏ ḫntj-š pr-ᶜ3 Jšfw* . . . 'the hereditary prince, the superintendent of the *ḫntj-š* officials of the palace, Ishfu . . .'.

The False Door

Pls. 17-19.

The door was found in five pieces in the main shaft. Because all its scenes and inscriptions are executed in bas relief, their surfaces have suffered great damage in the rough treatment to which this monument was subjected. The names and figures of the owner have been carefully chiselled out, but sufficient traces remain in various sections to allow the reconstruction of the name Ishfi. The door itself was painted in a pinkish colour, while some traces indicate that the hieroglyphs were painted yellow. Each third leaf in the cavetto-cornice is coloured yellow, while each fourth one is red.

Above the Cornice: *jm3ḫw ḫr nṯr ᶜ3 ḫr Jnpw tpj ḏw.f sḥḏ ḫntj[-š] pr-ᶜ3* . . . 'the honoured one before the great god and before Anubis who is on his hill, the superintendent of the *ḫntj-š* officials of the palace . . .'.

The Upper Lintel: (1) *ḥtp dj nswt ḥtp Jnpw ḫntj zḥ-nṯr tpj ḏw.f jmj wt* (2) *ḥtp dj nswt Wsjr ḫntj Ḏdw qrs.tj.f ḫrt-nṯr* '(1) An offering which the king gives and an offering which Anubis foremost of the divine booth, who is on his hill, who is in the embalming place (gives). (2) An offering which the king gives and Osiris foremost of Busiris (gives): that he be buried (in) the necropolis'. To the left a vertical line reads: *jmj-r st ḫntj[-š]* . . . 'the overseer of the department of the *ḫntj-š* officials . . .'. The name and representation of the owner are erased.

The Right Outer Jamb: (1) *ḥtp dj nswt prt-ḫrw [n].f m ḥb nb hrw nb m jm3ḫw* (2) *ḥtp dj Wsjr nb Ḏdw ḫp.f ḥr w3wt nfr(w)t* . . . '(1) An offering which the king gives. May an invocation offering come forth [for] him in every feast and everyday, as one who is honoured. (2) An offering which Osiris lord of Busiris gives, that he may travel upon the beautiful roads . . .'. Traces of a standing figure of the owner holding a staff can be seen despite the erasure.

The Left Outer Jamb: (1) *ḥtp dj nswt prt-ḫrw [n].f m ḥb nb hrw nb m jm3ḫw [ḫr] nṯr ᶜ3* (2) *ḥtp dj Jnpw nb t3 ḏsr ḫp.f ḥr w3wt nfr(w)t nt ḫrt-nṯr* '(1) An offering which the king gives. May an invocation offering come forth [for] him in every feast and everyday, as one who is honoured before the great god. (2) An offering which Anubis lord of the sacred land gives, that he may travel upon the beautiful roads of the necropolis'. The figure and the name are erased.

The Central Panel: To the right is a stand with jars and food containers. In the centre the tops of the bread loaves are visible, but the rest of the table and the figure of the tomb owner have been completely removed. The inscriptions at the top read: *jrj-pᶜt ḥ3tj-ᶜ*[16] *smr wᶜtj* . . . 'the hereditary prince, the count, the sole companion . . .'.

The Lower Lintel: (1) *špsj nswt jmj-r st ḫntj-š pr-ᶜ3 špsj nswt* (2) *sḥḏ ḫntj-š pr-ᶜ3 ḥrj-sšt3* . . . '(1) the nobleman of the king, the overseer of the department of the *ḫntj-š* officials of the palace, the nobleman of the king,[17] (2) the superintendent of the *ḫntj-š* officials of the palace, he who is privy to the secret . . .'. The name of the owner was chiselled out, but enough remains to suggest the reading of *Jšfj* 'Ishfi'.

The Right Inner Jamb: (1) *jm3ḫw ḫr nswt* (2) *jm3ḫw ḫr Wsjr* '(1) the honoured one before the king, (2) the honoured one before Osiris'. Traces of a standing figure holding a staff can be seen below a horizontal inscription . . . *ḫntj-š* . . .

The Left Inner Jamb: (1) *[jm3ḫw] ḫr n[sw]t* (2) *jm3ḫw ḫr Jnpw tpj ḏw.f* '(1) the honoured one before the king, (2) the honoured one before Anubis who is on his hill'. Only part of a title

. . . ḫntj-š remains, below which the surface is erased.

The Drum: This contained the name of the owner, of which the signs *Jš[fj]* can be seen.

NOTES

1. The name is not listed in Ranke, *Personennamen.*
2. Ibid 1, 47:6.
3. For discussion see *Saqqara* 1, 11-12.
4. Sethe, *Urk.* 1, 100:7-11.
5. Capart, *Rue de tombeaux,* pls. 34-35, 73; Badawy, *Nyhetep-Ptah,* figs. 33, 42, 45, 52.
6. Ibid, fig. 16; Capart, *Rue de tombeaux,* pl. 73; Strudwick, *Administration,* 67.
7. This could indicate that Ankhmahor was married twice, and that each of the two Ishfis was his eldest son by a different woman. (On the question of such eldest sons see Kanawati, *Chron. d'Ég.* 51 [1976], 235ff.).
8. Contrast Badawy, who considers the two to be one and the same person (*Nyhetep-Ptah,* 23, 50).
9. Compare, for example, the three eldest sons depicted in the same scene in the mastaba of Ptahhetep (Davies, *Ptahhetep* 2, pl. 24).
10. Badawy, *Nyhetep-Ptah,* fig. 33.
11. Ibid, fig. 52.
12. Capart, *Rue de tombeaux,* pl. 73; Strudwick, *Administration,* 67.
13. For example, *jmj-r prwj-ḥḏ* and *jmj-r šnwtj.*
14. For example, Khui (Drioton, *ASAE* 43 [1943], 502-504); Idu/Nefer (Junker, *Gîza* 8, 69ff.); Nekhebu (Strudwick, *Administration,* 113); and Hesi (see above).
15. For example, Memi (*Saqqara* 1, 27, pl. 11) and Ihyemsaf (ibid, 21-22, pl. 8).
16. *ḥ3tj-ʿ* is wrongly written as 
17. Notice the repetition of this title in the same line.

THE REUSE OF ISHFI'S MASTABA BY MESI

I THE TOMB OWNER AND HIS FAMILY

The Tomb Owner

NAME

Msjj[1] 'Mesi'.

TITLES

1 – *jmj-r ḥ3tjw* 'overseer of the foremost ones'.
2 – *špsj nswt* 'nobleman of the king'.

The Wife of Mesi

NAME

Jḫ̌rt[2] 'Ikhert'.

TITLES

1 – *ḥm(t)-nṯr Ḥwt-ḥr* 'priestess of Hathor'.
2 – *špst nswt* 'noblewoman of the king'.

The Son of Mesi

NAME

Gm-n.j[3] 'Gemni'.

II DATING AND IDENTITY OF MESI

A rectangular shaft is cut into the north-west corner of Ishfi's chapel, and extends further north into the narrow street in front of the tomb. The cutting of this shaft necessitated the removal of Ishfi's false door and entrance lintel, which were dumped in his own shaft. Above the rock level, the walls of the rectangular shaft were constructed with mud brick and stone pieces to a height of 1.70m., above which a wall was added on the west side, where the false door and the side panel of Mesi were placed, although when found, these had collapsed *in situ*.

The identity of Mesi is of particular importance, for it signifies the time when the alteration to the original mastaba took place. There is no indication in this part of the cemetery that officials usurped earlier tombs; and, indeed, Mesi did not reuse Ishfi's shaft, but rather cut his own, almost within the boundaries of the tomb and without blocking the entrance to its chapel. He also did not attempt to dispose of Ishfi's inscribed objects, but 'concealed' them in the burial chamber, which must have been accessible in his time. One wonders if Ishfi's shaft was ever used. The choice, or allocation, of this site for Mesi's burial place seems to have been influenced by some kind of relationship with Ishfi. In the tomb of Ankhmahor a man called Mesi is shown in a prominent position among family members, including Ishfi.[4] Although the name there is written as and the title 'scribe of the house of the sacred books of the palace' is not recorded on our small false door, the identification of the two individuals should at least be considered. The type of false door with a T-shaped panel does not in itself indicate a date at the end of Dynasty 6 or even later.[5] The earliest dated example of this type belonged to Pepydjedi, probably a son of Khentika, who added the door in his father's tomb later in Pepy I's reign.[6] Another example, presumably from the end of the same reign, belongs to the vizier Tjetju.[7] Four false doors are very close in type and in their proportions of height to width: the above-mentioned door of Pepydjedi, and those of Mesi, Nebemdjeri and Gemni,[8] this last being perhaps the son of Mesi.[9] This type of false door continued throughout the reign of Pepy II and beyond, but there appears to have been a return then to a more elongated shape.[10]

Suggested date: Late Pepy I.

III ARCHITECTURAL FEATURES AND IV BURIAL APARTMENT

See above, under the Mastaba of Ishfi.

V SCENES AND INSCRIPTIONS

The False Door

Pl. 20.

All decoration is in incised relief, with a little modelling only for the tomb owner's body. Four horizontal bands of colour extend across the door, beneath the drum: (from top) red, black, yellow and black. The owner's body is painted red-brown, while the central niche and both sides of the cornice are red.

The Top of the Frame: *ḥtp dj nswt Jnpw prt-ḫrw n jm3ḫw špsj nswt Msjj* 'An offering which the king gives and Anubis (gives). May an invocation offering come forth for the honoured one, the nobleman of the king, Mesi'.

The Upper Lintel: *špsj nswt jmj-r ḥ3tjw jm3ḫw Msjj* 'the nobleman of the king, the overseer of the foremost ones, Mesi'.

The Right Outer Jamb: *špst nswt ḥm(t)-nṯr Ḥwt-ḥr jm3ḫwt Jḫrt* 'the noblewoman of the king, the priestess of Hathor, the honoured one, Ikhert'.

The Left Outer Jamp: As on the upper lintel.

The Central Panel: The owner sits before a low offering table, on a chair without a back and with no front legs visible. Five *ḫ3* 'thousand' signs are written across the top of the panel, with the items inscribed below them. Although these are damaged, one can see the traces of *t* . . . *ḥnqt k3 3pd* 'bread, . . ., beer, oxen and fowl' *n jm3ḫw Msjj* 'for the honoured one, Mesi'.

The Lower Lintel: *jm3ḫw Msjj* 'the honoured one, Mesi'.

The Side Panel

Pls. 20-21.

This panel was attached to the left side of the false door, probably forming a kind of niche in which the door was placed. No other piece was found for the opposite side, which could have been formed by the brick chapel wall itself. The decoration is incised, with minimum modelling of the human figure, but clear details in the wig. The body is coloured red-brown, the skirt white, the bird's wings red and its body white. The lower part is decorated with bands, which correspond in position and colours to those on the false door.

The Inner Side: The upper section is occupied with offerings of bread, cuts of meat and jars of drink. In the lower section the son carries a bird in his right hand, while supporting with his left a vessel on his shoulder. Before him the inscriptions read: *z3.f mrjj.f Gm-n.j* 'his son, his beloved, Gemni'.

The Face: *ḥtp dj nswt Wsjr prt-ḫrw n špsj nswt jm3ḫw Msjj* 'An offering which the king gives and Osiris (gives). May an invocation offering come forth for the nobleman of the king, the honoured one, Mesi'.

NOTES

1. Ranke, *Personennamen* 1, 165:8.
2. Only the masculine form, *Jḫrjj,* is attested in ibid, 45: 13.
3. Ibid, 351:24.
4. Badawy, *Nyhetep-Ptah,* fig. 45. He is most probably the person with the same name and title shown in the chapel of Khentika (James, *Khentika,* pl. 10).
5. Strudwick, however, cautions against the early dating of these smaller tombs in the Teti cemetery (*JEA* 73 [1987], 277).
6. James, *Khentika,* pl. 42; Strudwick, *Administration,* 18.
7. Firth-Gunn, *Teti Pyr. Cem.* 2, pl. 61. For dating see Kanawati, *Governmental Reforms,* 35. The rejection of a date within Pepy I's reign (Baer, *Rank and Title,* 295 [576]; Strudwick, *Administration,* 161) is unjustified, since our knowledge of the titulature of this monarch's officials is far from satisfactory. The ranking of Hesi's titles, for example, does not fit in Baer's period VIB (*Rank and Title,* 234), yet the dating of this official seems almost certain (see above under The Mastaba of Hesi).

The ranking of Pepy I's officials should now be reconsidered in the light of new discoveries and progress in dating methods. The size and position of Tjetju's tomb does not preclude a date at the very end of Pepy I's reign, since there was a marked trend towards impoverishment of this monarch's officials (Kanawati, *Chron. d'Ég* 56 [1981], 206-209).

8. The doors of Nebemdjeri and Gemni were presumably added to the tomb of Tjetji shortly after its construction (*Saqqara* 1, pls. 23, 24).
9. A son named Gemni is depicted as the only offering bearer on the side panel of Mesi. If the identification of the two occurrences of the name is correct, then Gemni/Kagemni would have added his false door in the tomb of Tjetji, a relative (?). That Kagemni's false door is a later addition may be inferred from its position in the southern end of the chapel. In this group of tombs oriented N-S, the main false door, belonging to the tomb owner, was always situated at the northern end of the chapel.
10. See, for example, Firth-Gunn, *Teti Pyr. Cem.* 2, pls. 67, 70-74; Jéquier, *Particuliers,* figs. 98, 134, 138; Jéquier, *Monument funéraire* 3, figs. 60, 62-64, 70.

INSCRIBED OBJECTS AND FRAGMENTS

Several inscribed items were found in the 'fill' of compact earth and debris, filling the shafts and chapels and covering the mud brick mastabas to an average height of one metre above their roofs. Some items were also located in the loose sand which rose two to four metres above this level. The finds are divided into (A) complete objects and (B) fragments, and are listed according to the order in which they were recovered. References are made to the excavation number: S refers to Saqqara, followed by the year in which the object was found. In the case of complete objects this is followed by FD (false door), or OT (offering table). The last figure indicates the order in which the items were consecutively recorded. All inscribed objects and fragments are made of limestone. In the case of complete objects transliteration and translation of the texts are given, while only transliteration is provided of fragments as they are presently lacking in context. The great majority of these inscribed stones date to the Sixth Dynasty. When another date is suggested, it is given at the end of the entry. For the identification of a given location the reader is referred to the general plan on plate 1. With regard to measurements the following abbreviations are used: W=width; L=length; H=height. The excavated tombs were restored and locked, and were used as stores for all the portable finds from the excavation.

(A) COMPLETE OBJECTS

False Doors

S84:FD1. Pl. 22.

The false door of Kai, incised relief with minimum details. W. 58.5cm. H. 87.5cm. It is similar in type to those of Nebemdjeri, Kagemni[1] and Mesi (see above). Found in the fill of Shaft I of Iri (see General Plan, fig. 1).

The Top of the Frame: *ḥtp dj nswt Wsjr nb Ḏdw prt-ḫrw n jm3ḫw [ḫ]r* 'An offering which the king gives and Osiris lord of Busiris (gives). May an invocation offering come forth for the honoured one before' (text continues on the left of the frame).

The Left of the Frame: *Ptḥ-Zkr ḥq3 ḥwt smr wꜥtj ḫrp zḥ pr-ꜥ3 smr pr jmj-r . . . K3.j*[2] 'Ptah-Sokar, the estate manager,[3] the sole companion, the director of the food-hall of the palace, the companion of the house, the overseer of . . ., Kai'.

The Right of the Frame: *ḥtp dj nswt Jnpw ḫntj zḥ-nṯr prt-ḫrw n jm3ḫw . . . zš pr-ꜥ3*[4] *K3.j* 'An offering which the king gives and Anubis foremost of the divine booth (gives). May an invocation offering come forth for the honoured one, . . ., the scribe of the palace, Kai'.

The Upper Lintel: *ḥtp dj nswt Jnpw tpj ḏw.f jmj wt* 'An offering which the king gives and Anubis who is on his hill, who is in the embalming place (gives)'.

The Right Outer Jamb: *prt-ḫrw nt jm3ḫw K3.j* 'An invocation offering of[5] the honoured one, Kai'.

The Left Outer Jamb: identical to the right.

The Central Panel: Kai sits on a backless chair with lion's legs. He extends his left hand to an offering table, on the other side of which is a ewer. The inscriptions above him read: *ḫ3 t ḫ3 ḥnqt ḫ3 3pd ḫ3 k3 ḫ3 mnḫt jm3ḫw ḫr nṯr ꜥ3 K3.j* 'a thousand of bread, a thousand of beer, a thousand of fowl, a thousand of oxen and a thousand of clothes. The honoured one before the great god, Kai'.

The Lower Lintel: This is badly damaged, but its inscriptions may be restored as: *[jm3]ḫw ḫr* 'the honoured one before' (text continues on the left inner jamb).

The Left Inner Jamb: *Ptḥ K3.j* 'Ptah, Kai'.

The Right Inner Jamb: *ḫrp zḥ pr-ꜥ3 K3.j* 'the director of the food-hall of the palace, Kai'.

S88:FD2. Pl. 21.
The false door of Ked, incised relief. W. 33.0cm. H. 46.0cm. Found in the fill, one metre N. of Iri and at the latter's roof level. The crude style of the reliefs, the shape of the panel and the phonetic writing of Anubis suggest a later date than the original tombs in the cemetery, but not necessarily later than Dynasty 6.

The Top of the Frame: *ḥtp dj nswt Jnpw tpj ḏw.f prt-ḫrw* 'An offering which the king gives and Anubis who is on his hill (gives). May an invocation offering come forth' (text continues, with the repetition of *prt-ḫrw,* on both the right and left of the frame, which are identical).

The Right of the Frame: *prt-ḫrw n jm3ḫwt Qd*[6] 'May an invocation offering come forth for the honoured one, Ked'. The left of the frame is identical to the right.

The Central Panel: A crude representation of the owner is accompanied by the inscriptions: *ḫ3 k3 šs n Qd* 'a thousand of oxen and alabaster for Ked'.

S88:FD3. Pl. 23.
The false door of Hesut, incised relief. W. 28.0cm. H. 44.5cm. Found lying face down approximately one metre W. of Mesi. Probably close in date to S88:FD2.

The Upper Lintel: *ḥtp dj nswt Jnpw tpj ḏw.f* 'An offering which the king gives and Anubis who is on his hill (gives)' (text continues on the left outer jamb).

The Right Outer Jamb: *prt-ḫrw n jm3ḫwt Ḥzwt*[7] 'May an invocation offering come forth for the honoured one, Hesut'.

The Left Outer Jamb: *n jm3ḫwt Ḥzwt* 'for the honoured one, Hesut'.

The Central Panel: *ḫ3 t ḫ3 ḥnqt ḫ3 šs ḫ3 3pd(?) ḫ3 k3 n jm3ḫwt Ḥzwt* 'a thousand of bread, a thousand of beer, a thousand of alabaster, a thousand of fowl and a thousand of oxen for the honoured one, Hesut'.

The Lower Lintel: *jm3ḫwt* 'the honoured one'.

The Right and Left Inner Jambs: *jm3ḫwt Ḥzwt* 'the honoured one, Hesut'.

S88:FD4. Pl. 23.
The false door of Khnumhetep, incised relief, surface flaking and upper part missing. W. 63.0cm. H. 72.0cm. Found in the sand 5.5 metres N. of Tjetetu and one metre higher than the roof of this mastaba.

The Right Outer Jamb: . . . *[jm3ḫ]w jmj-r ḥwt-wr* . . . '. . . the honoured one, the overseer of the great mansion[8] . . .'.

The Right Middle Jamb: . . . *jmj-r pr mrjj nb.f [Ḫnmw]-ḥtp*[9] '. . . the overseer of the house, beloved of his lord, Khnumhetep'. A badly damaged standing figure of the owner is discernible.

The Right Inner Jamb: *jm3ḫw ḫr nṯr ꜥ3 Ḫnmw-ḥtp* 'the honoured one before the great god, Khnumhetep'.

The Left Outer Jamb: . . . *jm3ḫw Ḫnmw-ḥtp* '. . . the honoured one, Khnumhetep'. The sign  after *jm3ḫw* appears to be an error. The owner is depicted at the bottom, standing with his staff.

The Left Middle Jamb: . . . *qrs.t(j).f Ḫnmw-ḥtp* '. . . that he be buried, Khnumhetep'. The owner is represented standing and holding a lotus flower to his nostrils.

The Left Inner Jamb: *jm3ḫw ḫr nb.f Ḫnmw-ḥtp* 'the honoured one before his lord, Khnumhetep'.

The Central Panel: A very flaked scene of the owner at an offering table. He sits on a chair with lion's legs and a low back, placing his left hand on his chest, while extending the right towards the loaves on the table. Above the table are some cuts of meat.

The Lower Lintel: *jm3ḫw ḫr Jnpw* 'the honoured one before Anubis'. 'Anubis' is written phonetically.

S88:FD5. Pl. 24.
The false door of Kasedja, incised relief. W.

52.0cm. H. 90.0cm. Found face down in the fill of the inner court of Hesi's chapel, near the east wall and at a height of less than one metre from the floor. Although incomplete, the reliefs are of fine quality, and the type of false door is similar to that of Hesi.

The Upper Lintel: (1) *(ḥtp)*[10] *dj jn nswt ḥtp dj jn Wsjr*[11] *prt-ḫrw n špsj nswt* (2) *jm3ḫw ḫr Jnpw tpj ḏw.f nb t3 ḏsr K3-sḏ3*[12] 'An offering given by the king and an offering given by Osiris. May an invocation offering come forth for the nobleman of the king, (2) the honoured one before Anubis who is on his hill, lord of the sacred land, Kasedja'.

The Central Panel: The decoration on the panel is of cruder quality and obviously unfinished relief. The owner is depicted seated to the left of an offering table. On the opposite side of the table is a stand with three jars, above which are some food items. Above the table is written: *ḫ3 t ḫ3 ḥnqt ḫ3 3pd šs ḫ3 mnḫt* 'a thousand of bread, a thousand of beer, a thousand of fowl and alabaster, and a thousand of clothes'.

Offering Tables

S83:OT1. Pl. 24.
The offering basin of Iri. L. 20.0cm. W. 17.0cm. Two lines of crudely incised hieroglyphs: (1) *jmj-r ḫntj-š pr-ꜥ3* (2) *Jrj* '(1) the overseer of the *ḫntj-š* officials of the palace, (2) Iri'. Found in the fill west of Khui, half a metre above floor level, but it may belong to the tomb of Iri.

S88:OT2. Pl. 24.
The offering table of Kedut. Shaped as a *ḥtp* sign with two basins. L. 47.0cm. W. 24.5cm. Incised hieroglyphs: *jm3ḫwt Qdwt.*[13] 'the honoured one, Kedut'. This is followed by a seated woman determinative. Found immediately west of Ishfi, approximately one metre from floor level.

S88:OT3. Pl. 25.
The offering table of Kedet. Shaped as a *ḥtp* sign with two basins. L. 41.0cm. W. 27.0cm. Incised hieroglyphs: (1) *ḥtp dj*[14] *nswt Jnpw tpj ḏw.f jm3ḫwt Qdt*[15] (2) *prt-ḫrw nt Qdt.* 'An offering which the king gives and Anubis who is on his hill (gives), the honoured one, Kedet. (2) An invocation offering of Kedet'. Found in the fill of Shaft II in mastaba C, and may belong to the owner of false door S88:FD2.

S88:OT4. Pl. 25.
The offering table of Djefti. Shaped as a *ḥtp* sign with two basins. L. 35.0cm. W. 26.0cm. Incised hieroglyphs: (1) *ḥtp dj nswt Jnpw tpj ḏw.f prt-ḫrw n jm3ḫw(t) Ḏftj*[16] (2) *ḫ3 t ḫ3 ḥnqt ḫ3 k3 ḫ3 3pd ḫ3 šs ḫ3 mnḫt jm3ḫwt ḫr nṯr Ḏftj* '(1) An offering which the king gives and Anubis who is on his hill (gives). May an invocation offering come forth for the honoured one, Djefti. (2) A thousand of bread, a thousand of beer, a thousand of oxen, a thousand of fowl, a thousand of alabaster and a thousand of clothes. The honoured one before the god, Djefti'. Found in the mastaba of Hesi, in the fill of the room containing Tetiankh's false door, one metre above the floor level.

Obelisk

S84:178. Pl. 25.
The obelisk of Pepyankh. Base 10.0cm. x 6.5cm. H. 20.5cm. Incised hieroglyphs on one side: *jm3ḫw ḫr Wsjr Ppjj-ꜥnḫ* 'the honoured one before Osiris, Pepyankh'. Found in the fill of Memi's shaft.

(B) FRAGMENTS

S83:1. Pl. 26.
A block with the figure of Anubis in elaborate bas relief. W. 69.0cm. H. 37.0cm. Found in sand near the surface, W. of Tjetetu. New Kingdom.

S83:9. Pl. 26.
Part of three registers of an offering list in incised relief: (1) *z3ṯ(?) s[ḏt] snṯr, sṯj-ḥb, ḥknw, sfṯ, nẖnm, tw3wt, ḥ3tt-ꜥš, . . .* (2) *t-wt, t-rtḥ, ḥ[ṯ3], nḥrw, dptj, pzn, šns, t-[jmj-]t3, [ḫn]fw, . . .* (3) *np3t, mzwt, ḏsrt j3tt, . . ., [ḥn]qt, šḥpt, pḫ3, ḏwjw sšr, d3b, jrp sḫtj, jrp ꜥbš, jrp . . .*'. Below these, in bas relief, are the heads and hands of two male offering bearers and the title *jmj-r st ḫntj-š*. W. 43.0cm. H. 33.0cm. Found in the fill above Tjetetu.

S83:22. Pl. 27.
Part of a horizontal line of incised hieroglyphs: *smr.* W. (max.) 23.0cm. H. 15.0cm. Found E. of Tjetetu, below roof level.

S83:24. Pl. 27.
Part of a male figure carrying the foreleg of an ox, bas relief. W. 36.0cm. H. 16.0cm. Found E. of Tjetetu.

S83:26. Pl. 27.
Upper part of a male figure in bas relief, the left hand supporting offerings on his shoulder, traces of red colour on the face. W. 9.0cm. H. 14.0cm. Found in the sandy fill S. of Tjetetu and N. of Semdent.

S83:27. Pl. 27.
Badly weathered block with the remains of two columns of hieroglyphs: (1) . . . *m ẖrt-nṯr m ḫprw nb mrjj.f n k3 n zš nswt* . . . (2) . . . *n k3 n zš nswt.* W. 20.0cm. H. 41.0cm. Found near the last. New Kingdom.

S83:28. Pl. 27.
Remains of three deeply incised hieroglyphs. W. 36.0cm. H. 14.0cm. Found near the last.

S83:29. Pl. 28.
Remains of three vertical lines of hieroglyphs in bas relief: (1) . . . *m zmjt [jmntjt]* . . . (2) . . . *m wp rnpt Ḏḥwtjt* . . . (3) . . . *jr(?)* . . . W. 32.0cm. H. 15.0cm. Found S. of Tjetetu and resembles the reliefs on his façade.[17]

S83:30. Pl. 28.
Part of the lower half of a man and a woman, seated on a chair, bas relief. W. 48.0cm. H. 42.0cm. Found near the last.

S83:31. Pl. 28.
Part of a foot and staff, incised relief. W. 11.0cm. H. 9.5cm. Found near the last.

S83:32. Pl. 28.
The back of a male figure and the remains of two vertical columns of incised hieroglyphs: (1) . . . *špsj nswt* . . . (2) . . . *rt* . . . W. 24.0cm. H. 11.5cm. Found near the last.

S83:34. Pl. 28.
Two fragments in bas relief which fit together, with the head and shoulders of two female figures facing in opposite directions. To the left are the remains of the back of a chair and part of the seated figure. Total W. 33.5cm. H. 14.5cm. Found near the last.

S83:35. Pl. 28.
Part of a stela showing the owner adoring Osiris, with an offering table between them, bas relief. Remains of three columns of incised hieroglyphs: (1) . . . *Wsjr* (2) . . . *ḥq3 ḏt dj.f* (3) . . . *nfr wʿb(?).* W. 17.5cm. H. 18.5cm. Found near the last. New Kingdom, probably Dynasty 19.[18]

S83:38. Pl. 29.
Part of a male figure carrying the foreleg of an ox, bas relief. W. 13.5cm. H. 17.0cm. Found near the last.

S83:45. Pl. 29.
Legs and lower body of a male figure, outline roughly incised. W. 20.0cm. H. 35.0cm. Found in sand N. of Meru and Ankh.

S83:46. Pl. 29.
Part of a figure and offerings(?), sunk relief, traces of black and red paint on frieze. W. 52.5cm. H. 20.0cm. Found in sand N. of Meru and Ankh.

S83:48. Pl. 29.
Part of an offering table with loaves of bread, outline roughly incised, similar to S83:45. W. 14.5cm. H. 20.0cm. Found N. of Meru.

S83:49. Pl. 29.
Remains of a horizontal line of incised hieroglyphs: *ḫrj-ḥbt ḫ* . . . W. 9.5cm. H. 8.0cm. Found in the fill of Ihyemsaf's chapel.

S83:59. Pl. 29.
Remains of one vertical line of incised hieroglyphs: . . . *[jm3ḫ]w ḫr [nṯr]* . . . W. 12.5cm. H.15.5cm. Found in the fill between Tjetetu and Memi.

S83:60. Pl. 30.
Part of the head and upper body of a man with a shoulder-length wig and collar, bas relief with fine details. W. 6.0cm. H. 18.0cm. Found near the last.

S83:61. Pl. 30.
Part of a head wearing a fillet and streamer, bas relief with fine details. W. 11.0cm. H. 15.0cm. Found near the last.

S83:63. Pl. 30.
Part of a horizontal line of hieroglyphs in bas relief:  W. 10.0cm. H. 3.0cm. Found near the last.

S83:64. Pl. 30.
Part of the torso of a male figure holding a censer, bas relief. W. 22.5cm. H. 9.0cm. Found near the last.

S83:68. Pl. 30.
Remains of the lower part of a male figure and a vertical column of hieroglyphs: . . . *33s* . . ., unfinished bas relief. W. 20.0cm. H. 16.5cm. Found near Memi.

S83:70. Pl. 30.
Part of two horizontal lines of incised hieroglyphs: (1) . . . *[tpj ḏw].f [nb] t3 ḏsr* . . . (2) . . . *prt-ḫrw n(?) Mmj.* W. 25.5cm. H. 16.0cm. Found in the fill of Memi's chapel, perhaps forming part of an architrave above his façade.[19] (See also under S84:222, 223).

S83:74. Pl. 30.
The head and shoulder of a male figure and part of a horizontal line of hieroglyphs in bas relief: . . . *snṯr s* . . . W. 20.0cm. H. 17.0cm. Found near Memi.

S83:79. Pl. 31.
Part of an offering list in incised relief giving the name of six items in six lines: (1) *[b3]b3wt* (2) *[n]bs* ᶜ (3) *t-nbs* (4) *wᶜḥ* (5) *[ḥt] nb(t) b[nrt]* (6) *rnpwt(?) [nbt]*[20] W. 23.5cm. H. 10.0cm. Found in the fill between Memi and Tjetetu.

S83:80. Pl. 30.
Two raised arms of two offering bearers carrying trays(?) on their shoulders, bas relief. W. 14.0cm. H. 10.0cm. Found in the fill of Shaft I of Ihyemsaf.

S83:85. Pl. 31.
The torso and arm of a portly man poling a boat, bas relief. W. 13.0cm. H. 11.5cm. Found N. of Memi and Khui.

S83:86. Pl. 31.
Part of a face, bas relief with red paint visible on nose. W. 20.0cm. H. 20.0cm. Found near the last.

S83:103. Pl. 31.
The remains of two standing male figures facing right, sunk relief, separated by a vertical column of incised hieroglyphs: *ḫrp sḫt ḥtpt*[21] *Nj-R*ᶜ[22]. Traces of red paint on leg and arm of figures. The fragment fits on the right with S84:249 and, together with S84:163a-c, 249, 250 and 261, may belong to an architrave with repeated standing figures of the owner alone,[23] or with other persons[24] if fragment S84:250 belonged to the same architrave. The owner is represented a number of times facing right and other times facing left. W. 47.0cm. H. 35.0cm. Found in the fill of Irenakhti's chapel. Since many large pieces of this architrave were found in the area, one may assume that it came from a mastaba in the vicinity.

S83:105. Pl. 31.
The lower half of a male figure carrying a goose, bas relief. W. 14.0cm. H. 23.0cm. Found near the last.

S83:122. Pl. 32.
Four jars in a stand, incised relief. W. 16.0cm. H. 18.5cm. Found N. of Irenakhti.

S83:127. Pl. 32.
Part of a column of hieroglyphs in bas relief: . . . *ḫrj-sšt3 n* . . . W. 13.0cm. H. 26.5cm. Found N. of Irenakhti, and with S84:157 may form part of Iries' entrance (see below).

S84:157. Pl. 33.
Remains of two columns of hieroglyphs in bas relief: (1) . . . *jmj-r [s]t n[t]*[25] *ḫntj-š Jr[j].s* (2) . . . *jm3ḫw ḫr nṯr* ᶜ*3 jr[j.s]*. W. 19.0cm. H. 35.0cm. Found in the fill of Iries' chapel and may well be part of his entrance. However, the title inscribed on this fragment is not attested in the complete inscriptions of Iries' own chapel, although it is carried by Tetiankh who owns a false door in the antechamber of Iries.[26]

S84:163a. Pl. 32.
Remains of two standing figures in sunk

relief, separated by a column of incised hieroglyphs: . . . *ḥrj-sšt3 n nswt m [s]t[.f nbt].* Traces of red paint remain on the bodies. Fits on the left with the next fragment, S84:163b, and probably forms part of an architrave with repeated figures (see under S83:103). W. 36.5cm. H. 40.0cm. Found in the fill of Shaft I of Irenakhti.

S84:163b. Pl. 32.

Part of a standing figure in sunk relief between two columns of incised hieroglyphs: (1) . . . *sḥḏ ḥm-nṯr ḏd swt [Tt]j* . . . (2) . . . *jm3ḫw ḫr Wsjr [špsj] nswt* . . . Fits with S84: 163a (see above). W. 35.0cm. H. 43.0cm. Found near the last.

S84:163c. Pl. 32.

A hand holding a staff in sunk relief and part of a column of incised hieroglyphs: . . . *st* . . . May be part of the abovementioned architrave (see under S83:103). W. 8.0cm. H. 10.5cm. Found with the last.

S84:164. Pl. 33.

Part of a horizontal line of incised hieroglyphs: . . . *w jt jt(?)* . . . W. 8.0cm. H. 9.0cm. Found in the same shaft as the last.

S84:179. Pl. 33.

Remains of three columns of incised hieroglyphs: (1) . . . *zš Ptḥ-m-ḥ3t*[27] *m3ᶜ-ḫrw* (2) . . . *n Wsjr zš Ptḥ-m-ḥ3t m3ᶜ-ḫrw*[28] (3) . . . The fragment fits on the left with S84:238. W. 17.0cm. H. 38.0cm. Found above the NE corner of the roof of Mehi. New Kingdom.

S84:183. Pl. 33.

A male head in bas relief. W. 11.0cm. H. 18.0cm. Found in sand east of Mehi. New Kingdom.

S84:184. Pl. 33.

Part of two horizontal lines of incised hieroglyphs: (1) . . . *t* . . . (2) . . . *zm3* . . . W. 13.5cm. H. 11.0cm. Found in the fill of Shaft I of Irenakhti.

S84:195. Pl. 34.

Part of one column of incised hieroglyphs with traces of red paint: . . . *[jm3ḫ]w ḫr Jnpw [tpj] ḏw[.f]*. W. 7.5cm. H. 11.5cm. Found in the fill of Shaft I of Tjetji.

S84:205a-e. Pl. 34.

Five small fragments found together in Shaft I of Tjetetu. All may be parts of the same false door, together with S84:227. Incised hieroglyphs, with traces of red paint possibly in imitation of red granite.

(a) Part of cavetto cornice surmounted by a horizontal line of hieroglyphs painted in blue: . . . *n[sw]t Jnpw tpj ḏw.f prt-ḫrw.* W. 12.0cm. H. 10.0cm.
(b) Part of a door jamb with a column of hieroglyphs: . . . *špsj nswt Mrj*[29] W. 7.0cm. H. 15.0cm.
(c) Part of an inscription: . . . *špsj* . . . W. 6.0cm. H. 9.0cm.
(d) Corner of a torus moulding. W. 5.0cm. H. 12.0cm.
(e) The right side of a false door. W. 10.0cm. H. 14.0cm.

S84:208. Pl. 34.

Torso of a male figure facing left, behind him a set of jars with lotus blossoms on top, bas relief. W. 20.0cm. H. 13.5cm.

S84:209. Pl. 34.

Lower half of three men with offerings, facing left, in bas relief. W. 43.0cm. H. 16.0cm. Found in Shaft II of Tjetetu.

S84:211. Pl. 34.

Lower section of one horizontal line of incised hieroglyphs: . . . *f* . . . *n [q]rs[.tj].f(?)* . . . W. 83.0cm. H. 10.0cm. Found in the fill of a shaft E. of Tjetetu.

S84:212. Pl. 35.

Parts of two registers in bas relief representing (top) feet facing right and (bottom) male head and the sign *smsw.* W. 17.5cm. H. 11.0cm. Found with the last.

S84:213. Pl. 35.

An arm holding a staff, and the signs *z3.f ḫrj-ḥbt* in bas relief. W. 17.0cm. H. 17.5cm. Found with the last.

S84:222. Pl. 35.

Bottom of a column of incised hieroglyphs, painted in blue: . . . *mj,* perhaps Memi. W. 16.0cm. H. 34.0cm. Found in Shaft II of Mehi, but together with S83:70 and S84:223 may have formed part of the entrance to Memi's tomb.

S84:223. Pl. 35.
Part of a column of incised hieroglyphs, painted in blue: *ẖrj-ḥbt ẖrj-sšt[3]*. . . W. 16.0cm. H. 34.0cm. Found with the last and probably belongs with it to a door jamb.

S84:227. Pl. 35.
A section of a false door inscribed with incised hieroglyphs. Traces of red paint in imitation of granite. Lintel: *ḫntj-š Mrj*. Outer jamb: (1) *jm3ḫw ḫr nṯr ꜥ3 ḫr Wsjr nb* . . . (2) *jm3ḫw ḫr Jnpw tpj ḏw.f* . . . *m* . . . Inner jamb: (1) *ḏd swt Ttj* . . . (2) *jm3ḫw ḫr nswt jmj jb* . . . W. 32.0cm. H. 45.0cm. Found in the fill of Shaft I of Mehi. May belong with S84:205.

S84:238. Pl. 36.
A standing male figure supporting a mummy, probably in an 'opening of the mouth' ceremony, sunk relief. Two columns of incised hieroglyphs: (1) . . . *m3ꜥ-ḫrw* (2) . . . *Wsjr zš Ptḥ-m-ḥ3t m3ꜥ-ḫrw*. W. 45.0cm. H. 75.0cm. Fits with S84:179. Found in the fill above Mehi and Iri. New Kingdom.

S84:241. Pl. 37.
The lower half of three male figures facing left, and beneath them some roughly incised hieroglyphs: . . . *s, ?, w, t*. W. 55.0cm. H. 23.0cm. Found near the last.

S84:242. Pl. 37.
Part of an incised offering list with traces of green paint: Register I: . . . *t-wt, t-rtḥ, ḏsrt, ḥnqt-ḫnms, f3jt ꜥ (šns), šbw, swt, mw ꜥwj, bd, jꜥw-r šns ḏwjw, t-wt, t-rtḥ, ḥṯ3, nḥrw, dptj, pzn, šns, t-jmj-t3, ḥnfw, ḥbnnt, qmḥw qm3(?), jd3t ḥ3, p3wt*. Register II: . . . *[p]ḥ3, ḏwjw ssr, d3b, jrp mḥwj, jrp ꜥbšwj, jrp jmtj, jrp ḥ3mw, jrp snw, ḥbn(nw)t, ḥnfw, jšd, sḫt ḥḏt, sḫt w3ḏt, ꜥgt zwt, b(3b3)wt, nbs, t-nbs, ḥwꜥ (for wꜥḥ), ḫt nbt bnrt, rnpwt nb(t), ḥnkt nb(t), gsw pḫr, pḏw stpt, ḥ3t-wdḥw*.[30] W. 52.5cm. H. 26.0cm. Found in Shaft I of Mehi.

S84:243. Pl. 36.
Remains of one horizontal line of incised hieroglyphs: . . . 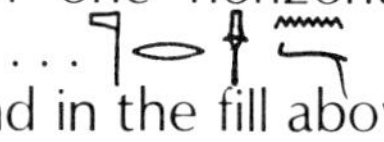 W. 38.0cm. H. 12.0cm. Found in the fill above Mehi and Iri.

S84:246. Pl. 37.
Part of the torso of a seated figure, bas relief. W. 45.0cm. H. 20.0cm. Found near the last. New Kingdom.

S84:249. Pl. 38.
Remains of two standing male figures in sunk relief with traces of red paint on the skin. In front of each a column of incised hieroglyphs: (1) . . . *? ḏd swt [T]tj jmj-r wpt ḫntj-š [Nj]-Rꜥ* (2) *jm3ḫw ḫr nswt m st* . . . Fits with S83:103 and probably forms part of an architrave with repeated standing figures (see under S83:103). W. 44.0cm. H. 44.0cm. Found in the fill above Mehi.

S84:250. Pl. 38.
Legs of a male figure with a woman standing behind him, sunk relief. May belong to the same architrave as the last. W. 17.0cm. H. 16.0cm. Found in Shaft III of Tjetji.

S84:251. Pl. 36.
Remains of four columns of hieroglyphs in bas relief: (1) . . . *ḫ* . . . (2) . . . *jm3ḫw ḫr P[t]ḥ* . . . (3) . . . *jm3ḫw ḫr Jnpw* . . . (4) . . . *s* . . . W. 43.0cm. H. 26.0cm. Found in the fill above Hesi.

S84:253. Pl. 38.
The torso of a male figure and the hand of an offering bearer wringing the neck of a goose, bas relief. W. 12.0cm. H. 15.0cm. Found in Shaft I of Tjetji.

S84:254. Pl. 38.
Part of one horizontal (1) and two vertical (2, 3) lines of incised hieroglyphs, possibly belonging to an architrave: (1) . . . *m ḫrt-nṯr j3w nfr wrt* . . . (2) . . . *ḫrt-nṯr* . . . (3) *špsj nswt smr pr* . . . W. 25.0cm. H. 30.0cm. Found in Shaft I of Mehi.

S84:255. Pl. 39.
Remnant of two incised signs, *jm3ḫ* and possibly *Jnpw*. W. 24.5cm. H. 10.5cm. Found in the fill of Shaft II of Tjetji.

S84:256. Pl. 39.
The torso of a male figure and the hand of another, bas relief. W. 11.0cm. H. 14.0cm. Found with S84:253 and probably belonged to the same tomb.

S84:257. Pl. 39.
Part of two horizontal lines of incised hieroglyphs with traces of blue paint: (1) . . . *[jmj w]t nb t3 ḏsr* . . . (2) . . . *m wp rnpt* . . . W. 20.0cm. H. 18.0cm. Found in Shaft I of Tjetji.

S84:259. Pl. 39.
Part of two horizontal lines of incised hieroglyphs: (1) . . . *m zmjt* . . . (2) . . . *Zkr* . . . W. 20.5cm. H. 12.0cm. Found in the fill above Hesi, but may belong to the same architrave(?) as the last.

S84:261. Pl. 39.
Part of a standing male figure in sunk relief and a column of incised hieroglyphs: *jmj-r swt šps(w)t pr-ʿ3*[31] *ẖrj-tp nswt jmj-r* . . . W. 16.0cm. H. 22.5cm. Found in the fill above Hesi and probably belonged to the architrave of *Nj-Rʿ* (see under S83:103).

S84:262. Pl. 40.
Part of one horizontal line of incised hieroglyphs with traces of blue colour: . . . *w3wt nfr(w)t n[t]* . . . W. 17.5cm. H. 7.5cm. Found in the fill above Hesi and may belong to the same architrave as S84:257, 259.

S84:263. Pl. 39.
Remains of two columns of hieroglyphs in bas relief, but only the signs
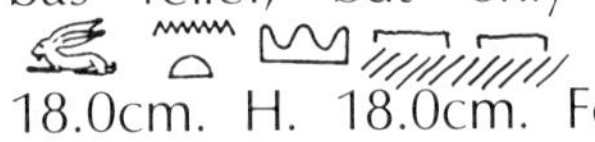
are recognisable. W. 18.0cm. H. 18.0cm. Found in the fill above Hesi.

S84:265. Pl. 40.
Two small fragments with incised hieroglyphs, one giving the name *Mḥ-n.s* and the other the title *jmj-r st ḫntj-š pr[-ʿ3]*. Found together near the last, but may belong to an architrave or a lintel of Mehi/Mehnes.

S84:270. Pl. 40.
The feet and lower part of the dress of a female figure, with incised hieroglyphs . . . *št*. These may refer to her name, possibly *Zšzšt*, which was common in this period. W. 16.5cm. H. 9.5cm. Found near the last.

S84:275. Pl. 40.
Part of a horizontal line of incised hieroglyphs with internal details: . . . *Jnpw tpj ḏw.f ḫrj-ḥbt Ḥwj*. W. 27.0cm. H. 14.0cm. Found near the last and probably belonging to the façade of Khui's tomb.[32]

S88:2. Pl. 40.
Fragment of a very lively boat-game in bas relief. W. 57.0cm. H. 29.5cm. Found in the fill of Shaft I of mastaba C.

NOTES

1. *Saqqara* 1, pls. 23, 24.
2. Ranke, *Personennamen* 1, 341:15.
3. For this title see Helck, *Beamtentitel,* 91, 113, 126.
4. See Junker, *Gîza* 3, 92, 97.
5. For similar writing see Firth-Gunn, *Teti Pyr. Cem.* 2, pl. 73:1; Simpson, *Qar and Idu,* fig. 32. The writing of *prt-ḫrw nt* offers another similarity with the false door of Nebemdjeri (*Saqqara* 1, pl. 23). For a recent study of this writing see Lapp, *Opferformel,* §68, 160ff.
6. Ranke, *Personennamen* 1, 337:6.
7. Neither the feminine, nor the triple writing of the *ḥz,* is attested in ibid, 255:10.
8. For a recent study of this title see Strudwick, *Administration,* 176ff.
9. Ranke, *Personennamen* 1, 276:6.
10. *ḥtp* is omitted.
11. For a recent study see Lapp, *Opferformel,* §47.
12. *K3(.j) sḏ3(w)* according to Ranke, *Personennamen* 1, 341:1.
13. Ibid, 337:18.
14. Although the formula may be read as *ḥtp rdj nswt* (Lapp, *Opferformel,* §26ff.), it is clear in this case that the *t* of *jm3ḫwt* is similarly written as *r*.
15. Ranke, *Personennamen* 1, 337:13.
16. The name *Ḏftj* is unattested by Ranke, although *Ḏf3t* and *Ḏfj* are listed (*Personennamen* 1, 406:21, 23).
17. *Saqqara* 1, pl. 14.
18. See, for example, Martin, *Ḥetepka,* no. 137, p. 44, pl. 39.
19. *Saqqara* 1, pls. 11, 12.
20. These are items 84-88 in Barta, *Opferliste,* 50, fig. 5.
21. This office may have had similar responsibilities to that of *jmj-r sḫtj ḥtpt (Saqqara* 1, 15, 19 n. 11).
22. Ranke, *Personennamen* 1, 172:23.
23. For references see Fischer, *Dendera,* 217-18.
24. Ibid, 218-19.
25. For the writing of this tittle as *jmj-r st nt ḫntj-š* rather than the more common *jmj-r st ḫntj-š* see Junker, *Gîza* 8, 51.
26. *Saqqara* 1, pls. 29ff.
27. Ranke, *Personennamen* 1, 140:1.
28. The rest of *m3ʿ-ḫrw* is found on fragment S84:238.

29. Ranke, *Personennamen* 1, 159:21.
30. For reading and meaning of these items see Barta, *Opferliste,* 48ff.
31. For this title see *Saqqara* 1, 37, pl. 22.
32. Saad, *ASAE* 43 [1943], 455-56; Drioton, *ASAE* 43 [1943], 502-504.

BURIALS AND FINDS

The distribution and type of burials found in the 1988 excavations at Saqqara followed the same pattern as those uncovered in the previous seasons' excavations (see *Saqqara* 1, 59ff.). The burials, generally in a decayed or fragile condition, were found, as before, at a height of 1.00m. to 6.00m. above the floor levels of the Sixth Dynasty mastabas. In the upper levels particularly, burials were placed directly in the sand and oriented in all directions, often with later burials cutting through earlier ones. Coffins were anthropoid or rectangular in form, two of the latter having domed lids.

Pottery, jewellery, cosmetic tools, scarabs and seals were found as isolated objects or accompanying the skeletal remains and coffins. While most of these were dated to the Eighteenth Dynasty, two Old Kingdom pots were found in the upper section of one of the Sixth Dynasty mastabas, and in the top metre of loose sand, two glass bottles from the Roman period. Dating of the finds has been tentatively proposed using stylistic comparison with other similar examples, and with information kindly provided by Dr. Colin Hope.

Each object is identified by its excavation number: S refers to Saqqara, followed by the year in which the artefact was found. The last figure is the consecutive order in which the items were recorded. In the measurement of the finds, the following abbreviations are used: H. = height; BW. = maximum body width; D. = diameter; Rd. = rim diameter; Bd. = base diameter; Id. = inner diameter; L. = length. All pottery is wheel-made unless otherwise stated.

BURIALS WITH FINDS

Burial 1. Approximately at roof level of the mastaba of Iri/Tetiseneb and 2.00m. north of this mastaba. A single, undisturbed burial lay with the head to the NW and facing west, the arms straight and the hands resting on the pelvis. The right foot was crossed over the left. The skeleton measured 1.65m. A pottery jar was found above the right shoulder next to the skull.

Finds: Pl. 41.

S88:2 – Wide-mouthed jar with convex neck, modelled rim and pointed base. White-coated Nile silt decorated on the neck and upper body with matt bands of black, red and blue.[1] H. 15.5cm. BW. 11.5cm. Rd. 9.0cm. Late Dynasty 18.

Burial 2. Pl. 47. 4.00m. north and level with the roof of Iri/Tetiseneb. A wooden anthropoid coffin lying E-W, measured 1.90m. long x .50m. wide. The face was well modelled and surrounded by a broad wig with long lappets. The eyes and eyebrows were painted in black. The skeleton, lying extended on the back with head to the west, arms straight with the hands resting on the pelvis, measured 1.64m. Two pots were found at the foot of the burial.

Finds: Pl. 41.

S88:16 – Single-handled drinking vessel with modelled rim and ring base.[2] Marl clay with greenish-white coating. H. 10.0cm. BW. 9.5cm. Rd. 7.5cm. Late 18th-early 19th Dynasty.

S88:17 – Open bowl with ring base. Cream-coated marl clay. H. 5.5cm. Rd. 14.3cm.

Burial 3. Immediately north of the mastaba of Iri/Tetiseneb and 1.00m. below the roof level of this mastaba. The burial was positioned NE-SW with the head of the coffin to the south. Most of the side and end walls of a rectangular wooden coffin remained, and contained a skeleton 1.70m. in length and .50m. wide lying with arms extended along the body. A Cypriote juglet lying close to the skull on its western side and a pottery jar were found with the burial.

Finds: Pl. 41.

S88:22 – Handmade Cypriote juglet with

inverted piriform body, trumpet-shaped base, single strap handle and slender neck tapering to a bell-shaped rim (Merrillees type BRI. IBa(ii)).[3] Black-coated Nile silt. Two horizontal relief straps around upper neck at junction of handle. H. 13.5cm. BW. 7.0cm. Rd. 3.5cm. Bd. 4.0cm.

S88:23 (not illustrated) – Large piriform jar with rounded base and modelled rim, broken into a number of pieces, very similar in form to S84:190 (*Saqqara* 1, pl. 46). Cream-coated marl clay decorated with three incised horizontal lines on the upper neck. H. 45.0cm. BW. 18.0cm. Rd. undetermined. Early-mid Dynasty 18.

Burial 4. 3.80m. north of the mastaba of Mehi and level with its roof. A double burial of an adult and a child was found surrounded by remains of the sides and end boards of a wooden coffin. The two skeletons were almost complete: the adult measured 1.65m. long x .40m. wide at the chest, while the child measured .75m. long x .25m. wide. The skeletons were both lying in an E-W position with the skull of the adult to the east and that of the child to the west. The child's skeleton was positioned above the right side of the adult with its skull approximately at the waist level of the adult and its feet resting on the skull of the other. Both had the arms crossed on top of the body with the hands over the pelvis. Scattered jewellery and remnants of a small wooden box were found near the skull of the child, togther with two pots.

Finds: Pl. 42.

S88:29 – Wide-mouthed, necked jar with modelled rim and ring base. Squat body with the bases of two horizontal(?) handles on shoulder.[4] Black-coated, burnished Nile silt. H. 7.0cm. BW. 11.5cm. Rd. 7.5cm. Mid-late Dynasty 18. The remains of a shattered, round-based Nile silt jar were found next to this pot.

S88:30 (not illustrated) – Remains of a wooden box consisting of: 2 pieces 10.0cm. x 3.5cm; 2 pieces 5.0cm. x 3.5cm. one of which was fitted with a domed knob measuring .8cm. in diameter; 1 piece 6.0cm. x 1.0cm. with a hole, .4cm. wide in diameter to take the shank of another knob; 1 knob, size and shape as previous example.

S88:31. Pls. 45, 49.

A. Rings

(a) Open-work, *wḏ3t*-eye ring[5] of turquoise faience. Bezel: 2.2cm. x .4cm. Id. 1.9cm.

(b) Mid-green faience ring formed of a cartouche inscribed with *Nfr-ḫprw-R*ᶜ, *w*ᶜ*-n-R*ᶜ (Akhenaten).[6] Bezel: 1.3cm. x 2.2cm. Shank: 1.8cm. x 1.6cm.

(c) Pale-green faience ring with bezel in the shape of a bulti-fish.[7] Bezel: 2.0cm. x 1.3cm. Id. 1.7cm.

(d) Oval, open-work ring with a Bes-image[8] holding a branch/vine(?). The bezel, 1.8cm. x 1.2cm., in yellow glaze with the shank in mid-blue glaze. Id. 1.6cm.

B. Beads

(a) A large number of pierced discs of blue faience, each .7cm. diameter.

(b) 3 pierced carnelian beads: 1 round, 1 bell-shaped, 1 cylindrical.

(c) 3 rectangular ridged pieces with loops at the top and the bottom: 2 dark blue, 1 red.

(d) 1 large and 1 small grey/white bead.

(e) 1 small, blue, round bead.

(f) 3 individual pendant beads: a mandrake fruit,[9] a lily[10] and a poppy-head.[11]

C. Blue faience face, 2.5cm. x 2.0cm. x .3cm thick, with carved features on one side only.[12] Late Dynasty 18.

S88:32 – Slightly to the east of this burial was found a slender, piriform Nile silt pot with a pointed base and a direct rim banded in black, which may be part of this burial. H. 15.5cm. Bd. 8.0cm. Rd. 4.5cm. Early-mid Dynasty 18.

Burial 5. 3.00m. north of the mastaba of Hesi and .25m. above the roof level of this tomb. Only fragmentary remains of a skeleton and a wooden coffin as well as a ushabti were recovered.

Finds: Pls. 46, 49.

S88:40 – Limestone, female mummiform ushabti, complete except for feet. Black, white and red paint on wig, face and body. Vertical column of inscriptions in black on front of figure. Extant H. 18.5cm. W. 6.0cm. Mid-late Dynasty 18.

Burial 7. Immediately behind, and parallel to, the north wall of the mastaba of Mehi and .50m. below its roof. A well-preserved skeleton, 1.60m. long, lay extended on its back with the head to the west and the hands resting on the pelvis. Some dark, plaited hair was still attached to the skull. Two pots were found with the burial: a large marl clay jar to the north of the skull and a Cypriote juglet near the feet.

Finds:

S88:44. Pl. 42. – Large, inverted piriform jar of marl clay, broken at rim and base, with a slender neck, concave in profile. Decorated on the neck with triangular or stylised petal forms, and at the widest point of the body with a black, undulating line. Both neck and body decoration are bordered in red.[13] Extant H. 42.0cm. Mid Dynasty 18.

S88:52. Pl. 43. – Handmade Cypriote juglet in red Nile silt covered in matt black slip. Inverted piriform body with two relief straps around the neck, single strap handle from upper neck to shoulder, trumpet-shaped ring-ware base (Merrillees type BRI.IBa (ii)). H. 15.0cm. BW. 7.5cm. Rd. 3.0cm. Bd. 3.2cm.

Burial 8. 3.00m. north of the NE corner of the mastaba of Mehi and .50m. below the roof level. A disturbed burial contained only fragments of bone, with a Cypriote pot and some cosmetic tools found near the skull.

Finds: Pl. 43.

S88:45 – Handmade Cypriote juglet of Nile silt with an inverted piriform body, tall, tapering neck, bell-shaped lip, single, strap-handle and low, broad base (Merrillees type BRII.IAa.). Decorated at the top and base of the neck, as well as at the widest part of the body with 4 horizontal bands in matt white, and around the upper body with groups of 4 diagonal lines crossing each other.[14] H. 14.5cm. BW. 8.0cm. Rd. 3.7cm.

S88:53 – 6 pieces of cosmetic implements, a portion of a wooden comb and the lower part of a metal phial:

(a) Oxidised metal phial, possibly the base of a kohl bottle. Extant H. 5.4cm.

(b) Kohl stick broken into 2 pieces. L. 11.5cm.

(c) 4 cylindrical pieces of wood, each approximately 3.0cm. long.

(d) Wooden comb. Measurements of remaining portion 2.8cm. x 2.0cm.

Burial 9. Pl. 48. 3.00m. above and 7.00m. NW of Tjetetu. A well-preserved skeleton, 1.65m. long with the head to the SE, lay with the head and shoulders elevated on a small mound of sand and rubble. The knees of the skeleton were raised at an angle and the arms were straight with the hands resting on the pelvis. Remnants of dark hair still adhered to the skull and fragments of woven wrapping material were found around the lower part of the skull and jaw, the wrists, knees and ankles. Behind the head was a wooden stick projecting to a height of .27m. above the skull, perhaps acting as a marker(?). At the base of this stick was found the broken base, .18m. high, of a conical pot containing traces of organic material.

Burial 13. Found in compact sand 4.50m. north of the NW corner of the mastaba of Mehi and slightly below its roof level. A wooden rectangular coffin with domed cover and decayed skeletal remains was positioned N-S with the head to the north. Two pots were found close by.

Finds: Pl. 44.

S88:59 – Large, red Nile silt pot with broken rim, no slip or other finish. Around the neck an incised line 5.0cm. below rim. Upper part of body smooth, but lower section towards base has turning incisions. Modelled rim, pointed base. H. 41.0cm. BW. 18.0cm. Rd. undetermined. Mid-late Dynasty 18.

S88:60 – Globular pot of red Nile silt covered inside and out with cream slip. Round base, narrow neck, collared rim. Decorated with blue, white, black and red horizontal and vertical lines on shoulder.[15] H. 17.0cm. BW. 12.0cm. Rd. 6.5cm. Mid-late Dynasty 18.

Burial 14. 3.00m. north of Mehi's mastaba and just above its roof level. The side boards of a wooden coffin with a skeleton in poor condition were found lying NE-SW with the head to the north. A large pot was found at the SE corner of the coffin.

Find: Pl. 44.

S88:61 – Fine-textured, Nile silt pot covered with red slip. Piriform body with a tall, concave neck and modelled but flattened lip, broken rim.[16] Decorated with black lines around the body and neck, with two incised lines on the neck. H. 43.0cm. BW. 22.0cm. Rd. undetermined. Thutmose III.

Burial 15. In loose sand 4.50m. north of Mehi and 1.00m. above the roof level of this mastaba. Fragments of a wooden anthropoid coffin and disturbed skeleton lying N-S. One seal was recovered from the burial.

Find: Pls. 45, 49.

S88:75 – Seal in deep blue faience, pierced longitudinally. Inscribed on one side with the epithet, *ptpt ḫ3swt* 'one who tramples foreign lands' and the cartouche of *Mn-ḫprw-Rᶜ*[17] (Thutmose IV). The figure of the god Ptah, holding a *w3s*-sceptre, is incised on the reverse. 1.6cm. x 1.2cm. x .5cm.

Burial 16. .50m. north and 1.00m. above the false door of Tetiankh in the mastaba of Hesi. The remnants of a wooden coffin and a skeleton were found together with one pot.

Find: Pl. 44.

S88:74 – Wide-mouthed, round-bodied pot of finely textured Nile silt covered with red slip. H. 11.5cm. BW. 13.0cm. Rd. 9.5cm. Dynasty 18.

Burial 17. 1.00m. north of the false door of Tetiankh and 1.00m. above it, in the mastaba of Hesi. In loose sand disturbed skeletal remains were found with a number of scarabs, amulets and beads.

Finds: Pls. 46, 49.

S88:76

(a) Open-work amulet of turquoise faience with a barrel-shaped suspension loop. Two baboons or figures of the goddess Taweret face each other on either side of a central, plant-like motif. 3.0cm. x 2.3cm.

(b) Scarab, pierced laterally, inscribed on the reverse with the prenomen of Amenhotep III *(Nb-m3ᶜt-Rᶜ)* and *nfr Ptḥ mr*[18] 2.0cm. x 1.5cm.

(c) Seal of blue faience, pierced laterally with the nomen of Amenhotep III on one side and the prenomen on the other. 1.8cm. x 1.3cm.

(d) Glazed bead with suspension hole, in deep blue and pale yellow.[19] 2.2cm. x 1.0cm. Amenhotep III.

(e) Bead pierced laterally in the shape of an *jb*-sign, made of black glass with horizontal white threads.[20] 2.0cm. x 1.5cm.

(f) 2 beads of blue faience carved on one side with the figure of Taweret, with a barrel-shaped suspension loop. 2.2cm. x 1.0cm.

(g) 1 damaged green faience pendant amulet of the figure of Bes, with a barrel-shaped suspension loop. 1.8cm. x .8cm.

(h) 7 pendant fish shapes, 3 red, 3 blue, 1 green, all of faience and modelled on 1 side only, each with a barrel-shaped suspension loop. 1.7cm. x .6cm.

(i) 1 blue tear-drop shaped bead with barrel-shaped suspension loop. 1.3cm. x .4cm.

BURIALS WITHOUT FINDS

Burial 10. Pl. 47. In loose sand 3.00m. above and 10.00m. north of the mastaba of Tjetetu. A wooden anthropoid coffin, measuring 1.87m. long x .47m. wide at the shoulders, was positioned E-W with the head to the west. It was covered with a thin layer of white plaster and decorated on the body in red, blue and black. The modelled face was painted pink with eyes and brows in black, framed by a white wig with tresses indicated by blue and red lines. The coffin had been completely broken through the centre by a later burial. This later skeleton, 1.58m. long, lay extended on its back at the same level of the coffin but at right angles to it. The lower leg bones were crossed and one arm was extended beside the body while the other was bent at the elbow with the forearm resting on the rib-cage.

Burial 12. Pl. 48. 5.00m. to the north and 2.50m. above the roof of the mastaba of Mehi. Four unpainted anthropoid wooden coffins lying almost parallel to each other were positioned with the head to the SW. The two coffins closest to the mastaba of Mehi were almost complete, measuring 1.70m. and 1.85m. in length. Of the remaining two only the upper sections had been preserved, measuring 1.50m. and 1.00m. All the coffins, together with the skeletons, had been crushed. However, the strongly- modelled face masks were intact, two of which had long, curving beards.

FINDS

JEWELLERY

S88:12. Pls. 45, 49.
Blue faience seal, inscribed with *mr-Jmn-R*ᶜ on one side and with a recumbent lion on the other. Found to the west and at the roof level of the mastaba of Mehi. 1.0cm. x .7cm.

S88:50. Pls. 45, 49.
Green faience ring with the cartouche of *Nb-ḫprw-R*ᶜ (Tutankhamun). Found in loose sand 5.00m. north of Tjetetu and approximately 1.50m. above the roof level of this mastaba. Bezel: 2.0cm. x 1.0cm. Id. 1.6cm.

S88:62. Pl. 45.
Open-work, pierced amulet in turquoise faience of a winged serpent and an eye within a rectangular frame. Found in loose sand 5.00m. north of the western wall of the mastaba of Hesi. 3.0cm. x 2.5cm. x .5cm. thick.

S88:71. Pls. 45, 49.
Found in loose sand 2.00m. north of Tjetetu and just below the roof level of this mastaba.
(a) A large number of small pierced discs of faience.
(b) Carnelian scarab. 1.2cm. x .8cm.
(c) Worn faience scarab, with *W3ḏt* incised on the reverse.

S88:72. Pls. 45, 49.
Turquoise faience scarab with the cartouche of Queen Tye on the reverse.[21] Found 2.00m. north of Tjetetu and at the roof level of this mastaba. 1.7cm. x 1.2cm.

GLASS

S88:69. Pl. 41.
Green glass tear bottle (lachrymoria) broken at neck, base slightly concave.[22] Extant H. 10.5cm. Bd. 4.5cm. Roman.

S88:25. Pl. 41.
Green glass lachrymoria[23] with flat base, tall, straight neck and uneven, flat lip, folded on the undersurface. Found in loose sand, 3.00m. west and 1.00m. above the mastaba of Hesi. H. 14.0cm. Bd. 4.0cm. Rd. 2.4cm.

STONE

S88:24. Pl. 46.
Limestone ushabti figure. H. 9.5cm. W. 2.2cm.

POTTERY

S88:1. Pl. 41.
Pale-coated Nile silt jar with neck and rim missing. Inverted piriform body, decorated on shoulder with three bands of matt blue. Found 1.00m. to the north and at the roof level of the mastaba of Mehi. Extant H. 24.0cm. BW. 19.0cm.

S88:9. Pl. 41.
Wide-mouthed, fine-textured Nile silt jar with a direct, slightly flaring lip and a rounded base. Covered with a thin wash of cream slip on the outer surface and the inside of the neck for .5cm. Decorated on the neck and body to 5.5cm. above the base with motifs painted in matt blue and red-brown, outlined in black. The motifs are divided into two panels separated by papyrus stands and *wḏ3t*-eyes. The major panel contains the figure of *ḥḥ* with *nb*, *ḏd*, ᶜ*nḫ* and *nfr* signs. The reverse panel shows bands of mandrake fruits and lotus buds and flowers.[24] The vase was found in several pieces 3.00m. north of the mastaba of Iri/Tetiseneb at the level of its roof. H. 26.5cm. BW. 16.5cm. Rd. 12.0cm. Amenhotep III or later.

S88:21. Pl. 42.
Broad-necked jar of Nile silt, broken at rim, convex neck and inverted, piriform body. Found 1.00m. to the north of Mehi's mastaba and at its roof level. Extant H. 33.0cm. BW. 24.0cm. Late Dynasty 18-early Dynasty 19.

S88:27. Pl. 42.
Coarse Nile silt jar with single handle, cylindrical neck and direct rim, ring-based. Cream slip on neck and shoulder. Found in loose sand 2.00m. north and 2.50m. above the roof level of the mastaba of Hesi. H. 15.0cm. BW. 10.0cm. Rd. 4.5cm. Bd. 5.0cm. Ptolemaic-Roman.

S88:28. Pl. 42.
As S88:27, but without slip. H. 13.0cm. BW. 11.0cm. Rd. 5.0cm. Bd. 5.5cm.

S88:36. Pl. 42.
Wide-mouthed Nile silt jar with a cylindrical neck expanding slightly to a direct rim, rounded body and base. Found 1.00m. to the north and .50m. above the existing wall height of the mastaba of Hesi. H. 12.0cm. BW. 10.0cm. Rd. 7.5cm. Mid-late Dynasty 18.

S88:38. Pl. 42.
Piriform jar of Nile silt coated with red slip and decorated with two incised lines below a modelled rim, rounded base.[25] Found .50m. to the north and .50m. above the roof level of the mastaba of Hesi. H. 16.0cm. BW. 11.0cm. Rd. 7.5cm. Early-mid Dynasty 18.

S88:43. Pl. 42.
Jar with broken rim and neck, of Nile silt with rounded body, flaring neck and direct rim. Found to the north of Iri/Tetiseneb and .50m. below the roof level of this mastaba. H. 14.0cm. BW. 10.0cm. Rd. 5.5cm. Dynasty 18-19.

S88:46. Pl. 41.
Miniature dish of Nile silt with flat base. Found 1.50m. north and .50m. below the present roof level of the mastaba of Mehi. Rd. 5.3cm. Bd. 4.0cm.

S88:49. Pl. 42.
Piriform jar of fine-textured Nile silt coated with red slip. Tall neck defined by a flat band 1.5cm. wide, below the modelled rim. Found 2.50m. north and .50m. above the mastaba of Iri/Tetiseneb. H. 17.5cm. BW. 7.0cm. Rd. 4.5cm. Late Dynasty 18.

S88:54. Pl. 43.
Piriform jar with pointed base and flaring rim.[26] Marl clay coated with red slip, with a 1.0cm. band of black paint defining the rim. Found 1.00m. to the north and .50m. below the roof level of Mehi. H. 21.0cm. BW. 13.5cm. Rd. 8.0cm. Early-mid Dynasty 18.

S88:57. Pl. 43.
Handmade cylindrical jar of coarse Nile silt coated with red slip. Found 2.00m. north and .50m. below the roof level of the mastaba of Mehi. H. 27.0cm. BW. 13.5cm. Rd. 12.0cm. Late Old Kingdom.

S88:58. Pl. 43.
As S88:57. H. 29.0cm. BW. 13.0cm. Rd. 12.0cm.

S88:64. Pl. 44.
Pot with rounded body, slightly pointed base, flaring direct rim.[27] Nile silt coated with red slip. Found 1.50m. north and .50m. above the mastaba of Hesi. H. 21.0cm. BW. 15.0cm. Rd. 10.5cm. Late Dynasty 18.

S88:65. Pl. 43.
Open dish of red-coated Nile silt. Decorated at rim with a black band. Straight sides, direct rim, disc base. Found 3.00m. north and .50m. above the roof level of Mehi. H. 5.0cm. Rd. 14.5cm. Bd. 3.0cm. Mid Dynasty 18.

S88:66. Pl. 43.
Open bowl of Nile silt, coated in red slip on inside. Direct rim, disc base. Found 3.00m. north and 1.00m. below the roof of Mehi. H. 5.0cm. Rd. 21.0cm. Bd. 7.0cm. Mid Dynasty 18.

S88:67. Pl. 41.
Miniature dish of Nile silt, with flat base. Found at a depth of 1.00m. in Shaft II of Mastaba C. H. 1.3cm. Rd. 4.0cm. Bd. 2.5cm. Late Old Kingdom.

S88:70. Pl. 44.
Inverted piriform jar with cylindrical neck,

direct rim and recessed foot. The base of a single handle remains below the rim. H. 13.0cm. BW. 10.0cm. Rd. 4.5cm.

NOTES

1. S88:1, S88:2, S88:9 are examples of the Blue-painted pottery produced from mid Eighteenth Dynasty until Dynasty 20. Bands of matt blue, black and red formed the most frequent decorative treatment, but floral motifs, bird and animal forms were also employed. See Bourriau, *Umm el-Ga'ab,* nos. 145, 152; Hope, *Céramique* 1, [1987], pls. 32-37.
2. See *Ägyptens Aufstieg,* 258, no. 185, from Tell el-Amarna; *Keramik* 169, no. 271.
3. Base Ring Ware I, two examples of which were found this season at Saqqara, S88:22 and S88:52, was introduced into Egypt by Cypriote merchants during the Second Intermediate Period (Merrillees, *Pottery,* 148ff.). This ware was replaced by Base Ring Ware II during the reign of Hatshepsut (ibid, 175ff.); see S88:45.
4. See Hayes, *Scepter* 2, fig. 123, for a similar pot with complete stirrup-like handles; Frankfort-Pendlebury, *Akhenaten* 2, pl. 53, no. 22.
5. *Golden Age,* 249, nos. 346, a-d.
6. Hayes, *Scepter* 2, fig. 180; Petrie, *Scarabs,* 43.
7. Samson, *Amarna,* 79, pl. 46; Petrie, *Amarna,* pl. 17.
8. *Golden Age,* 249, no. 345; Petrie, *Amarna,* 180, pl. 16.
9. For the use of this motif in a similar pendant form in a collar, see *Golden Age,* 234, no. 308; and on a faience tile from Amarna, Riefstahl, *Glass,* pl. 6, no. 28.
10. Petrie, *Amarna,* pl. 19, nos. 461-462.
11. Ibid, pl. 19, nos. 470-473.
12. Samson, *Amarna,* 45, pl. 45(ii); Riefstahl, *Glass,* 44, no. 43; Cooney, *Glass,* 85, no. 936.
13. See Bourriau, *Umm el-Ga'ab,* 77, no. 145, for a storage jar of similar shape and stylised petal/leaf forms on neck; also, Hope, *Ancient Egyptian Pottery,* pl. 11, no. 47.
14. For similar decoration see n.3, and Merrillees, *Pottery,* pl. 22, no. 4; pl. 23, nos. 4 and 5.
15. For a similar globular flask, decorated in blue and red and dated to the reign of Amenhotep III, see Bourriau, *Umm el-Ga'ab,* 73, no. 137.
16. Petrie-Brunton, *Sedment* 2, pl. 60.
17. For the use of the epithet see Newberry, *Scarabs,* pl. 28, no. 10; Petrie, *Scarabs,* 36, no. 1132. For a similar depiction with Ptah see Newberry, *Scarabs,* pl. 29, no. 42.
18. Ibid, pl. 30, no. 30.
19. See Cooney, *Glass,* 95, nos. 1019-1020, for two similar pomegranate-shaped beads.
20. Ibid, 16, no. 150. Glass objects appear for the first time shortly after the beginning of Dynasty 18, with only a few small objects, chiefly beads, being dated earlier than the reign of Thutmose I (Riefstahl, *Glass,* 4).
21. Petrie, *Scarabs,* 42, no. 1291.
22. Cooney, *Glass,* 100, no. 1051.
23. Ibid, 100-101, no. 1053.
24. For a similar representation of the *ḥḥ*-figure see BM47380, in Hope, *Pottery,* fig. 17. For shape and depiction of bands of lotus-flowers and buds, see *Keramik,* 158, no. 239.
25. Bourriau, *Umm el-Ga'ab,* 19, no. 8.
26. Peet, *Abydos* 2, pls. 12, 13.
27. Petrie-Brunton, *Sedment* 2, pl. 65.

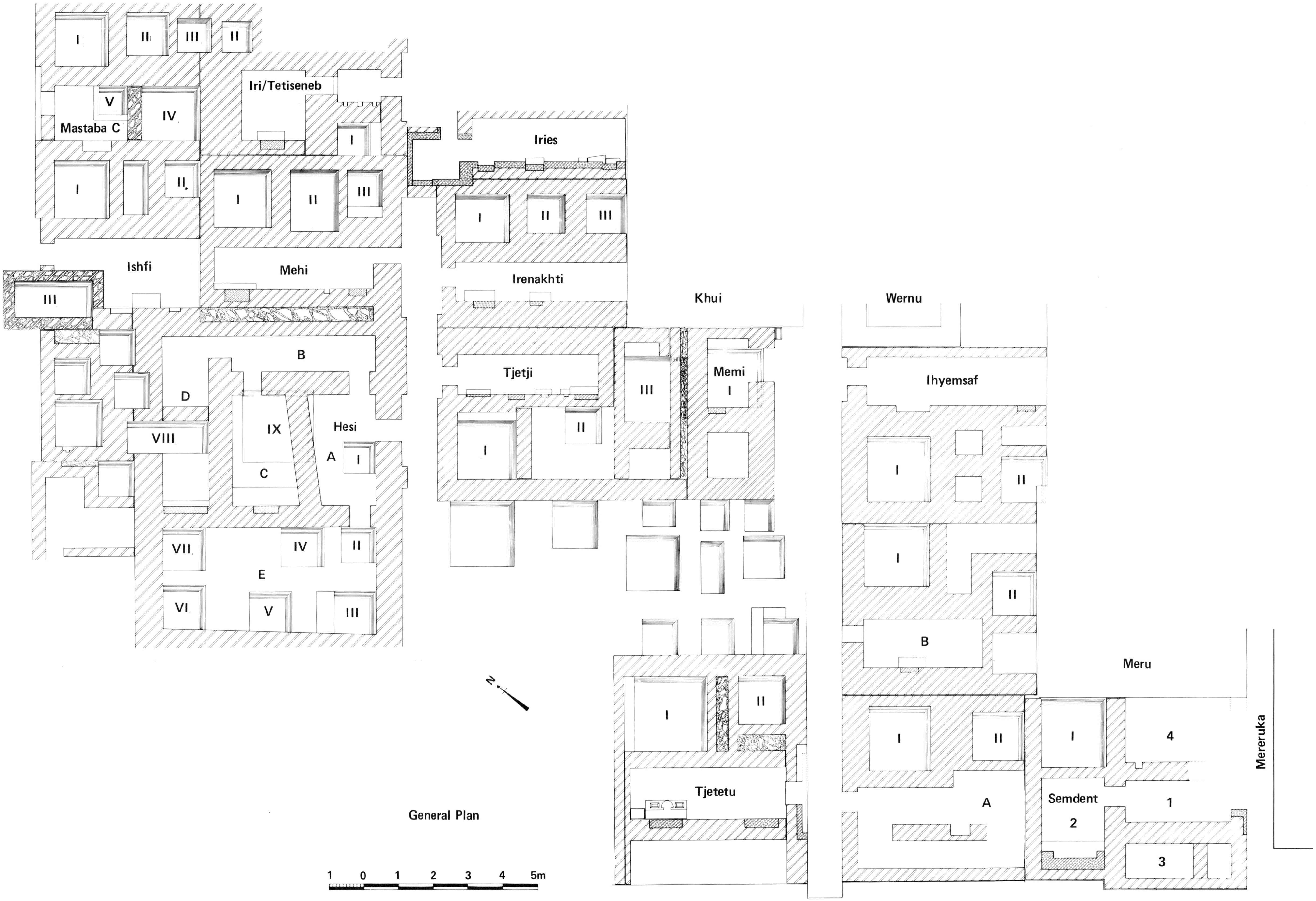

General Plan

Plate 1

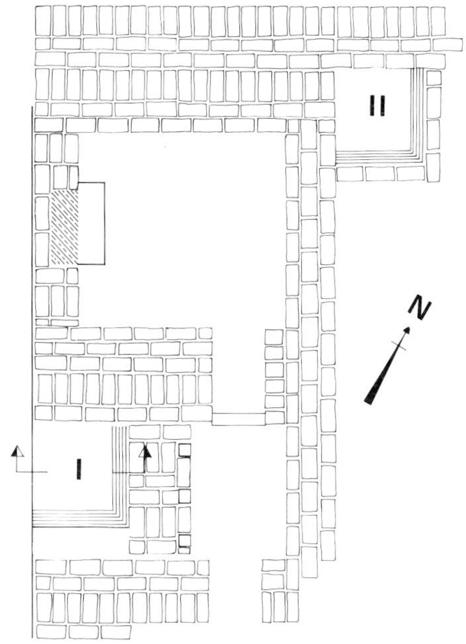

Plan

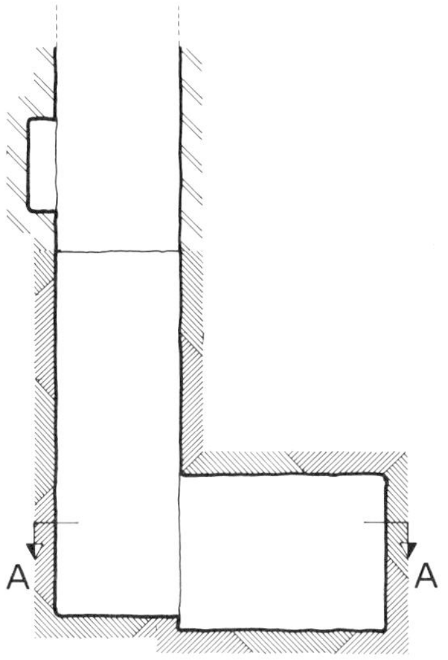

Shaft I

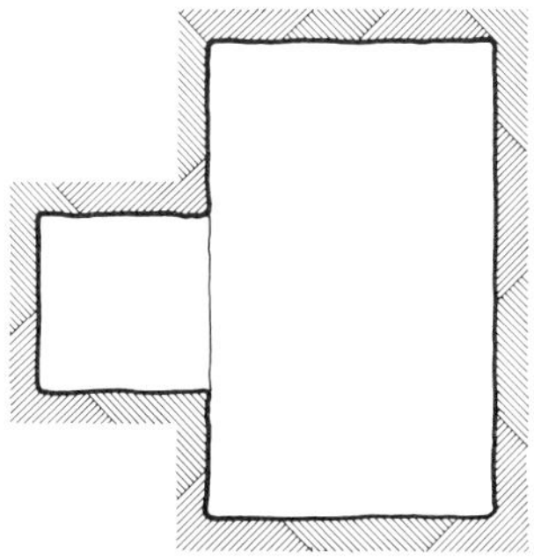

Section Plan A-A

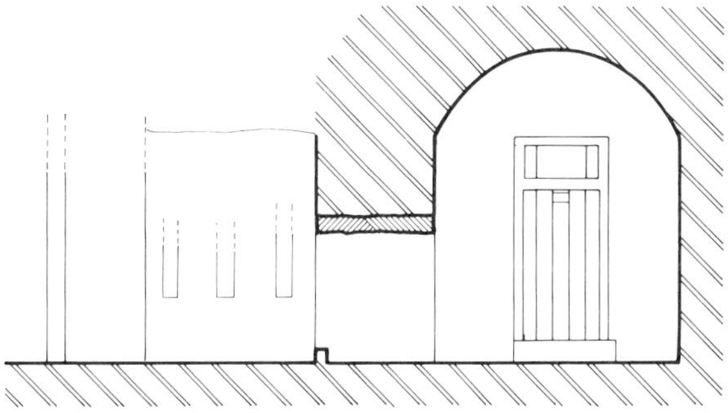

North - South Section Elevation

The Mastaba of Iri/Tetiseneb

Plate 2

Iri, architrave

Iri, lintel

Plate 3

Iri, false door

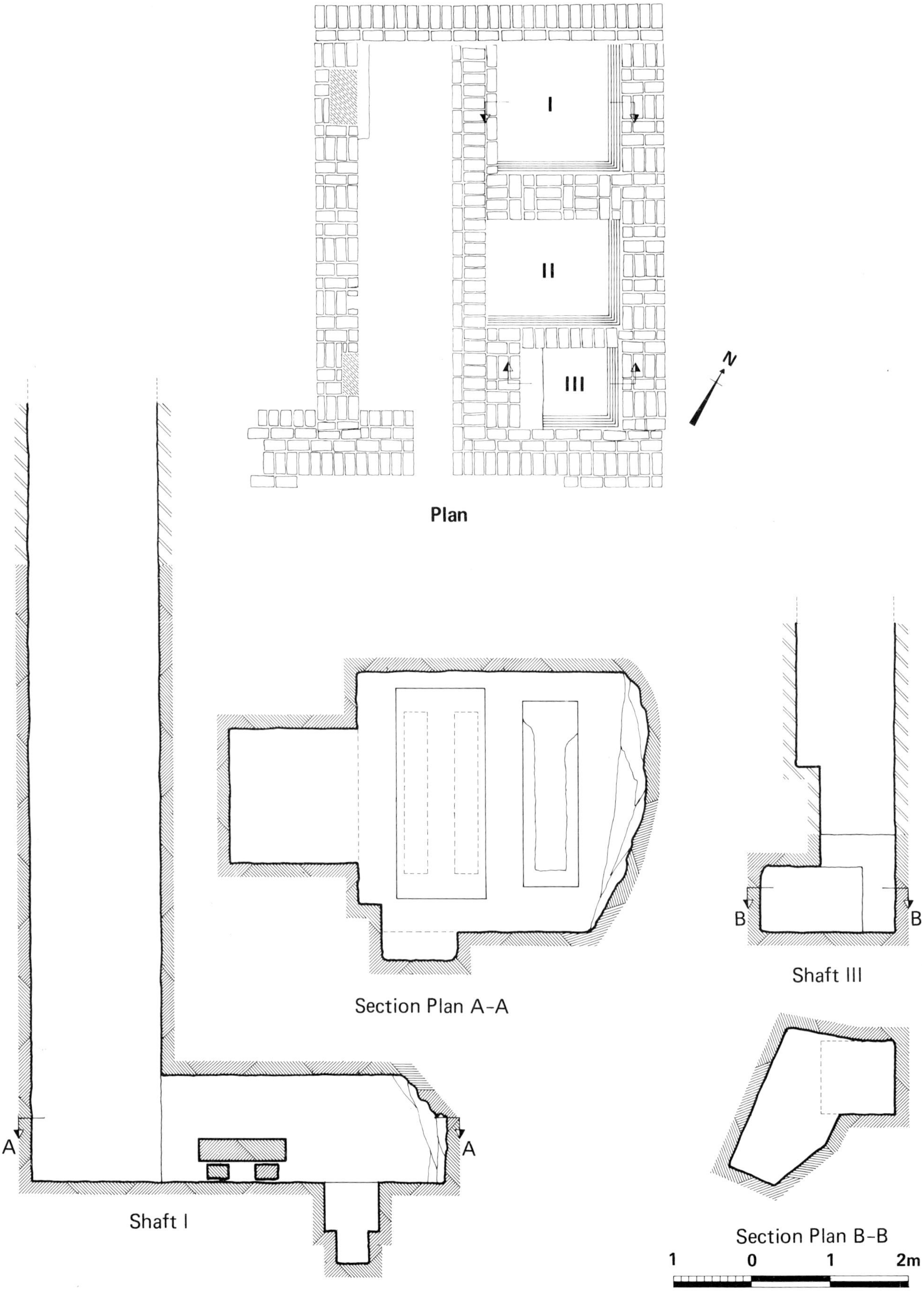

The Mastaba of Mehi

Plate 5

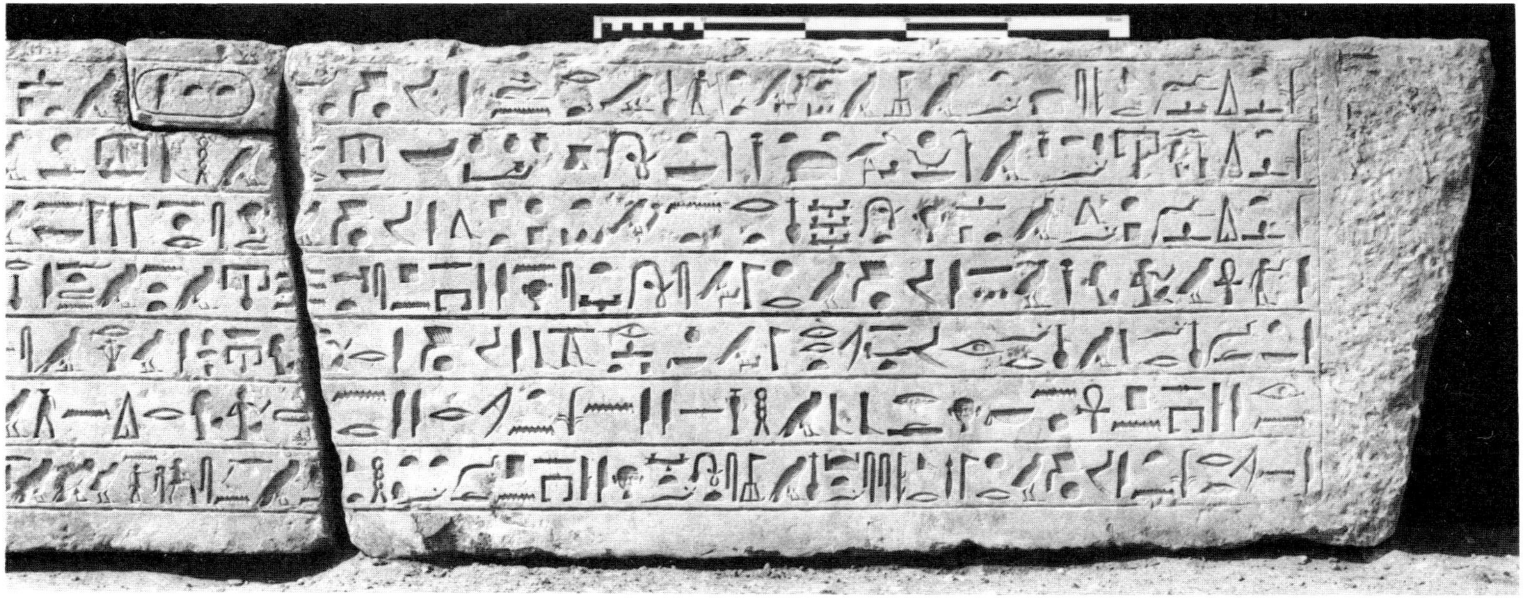

Mehi, architrave

Mehi, false door

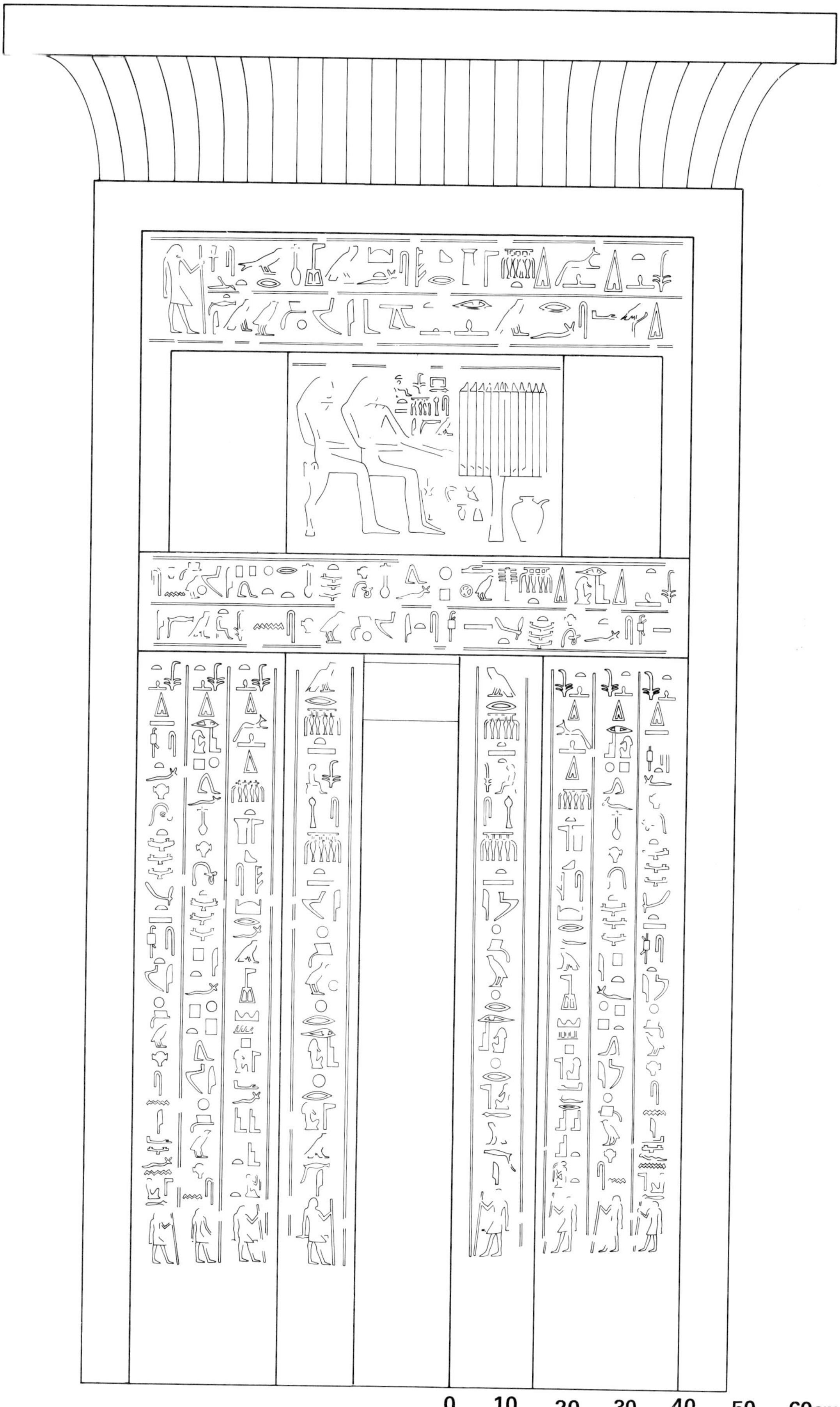

0 10 20 30 40 50 60cm

Mehi, false door

Mehi, chapel, false door of Khenti

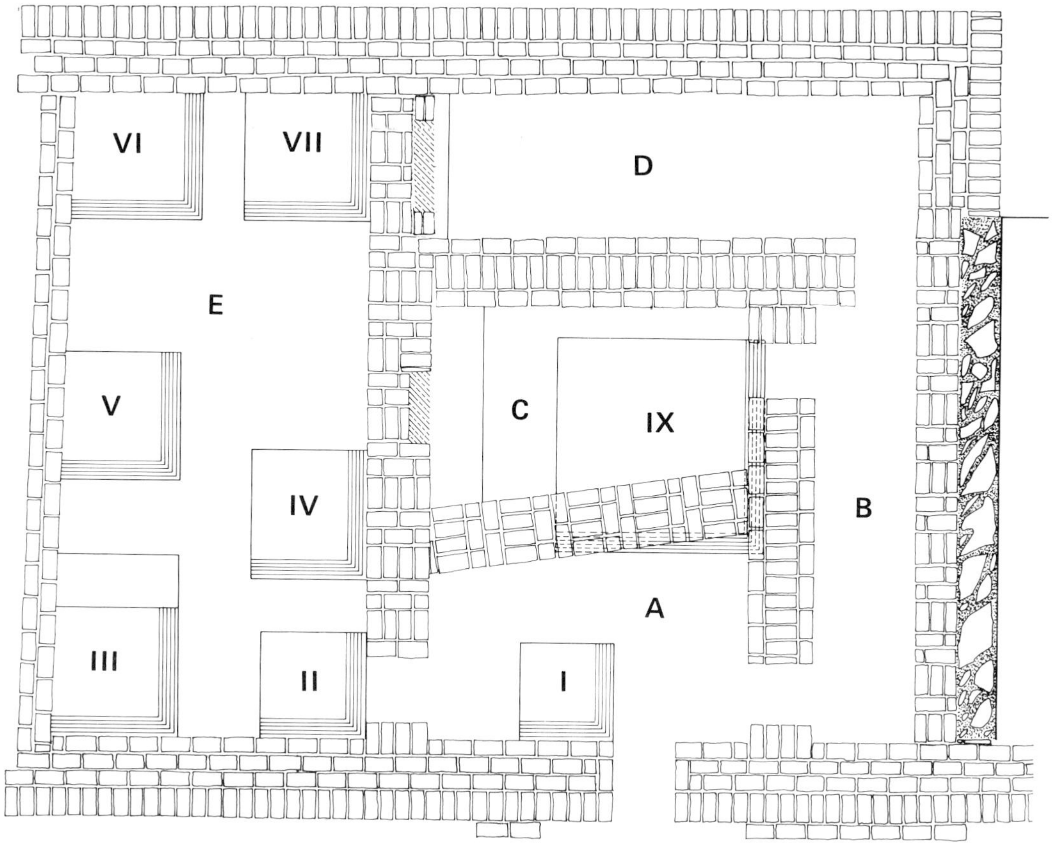

Original Plan

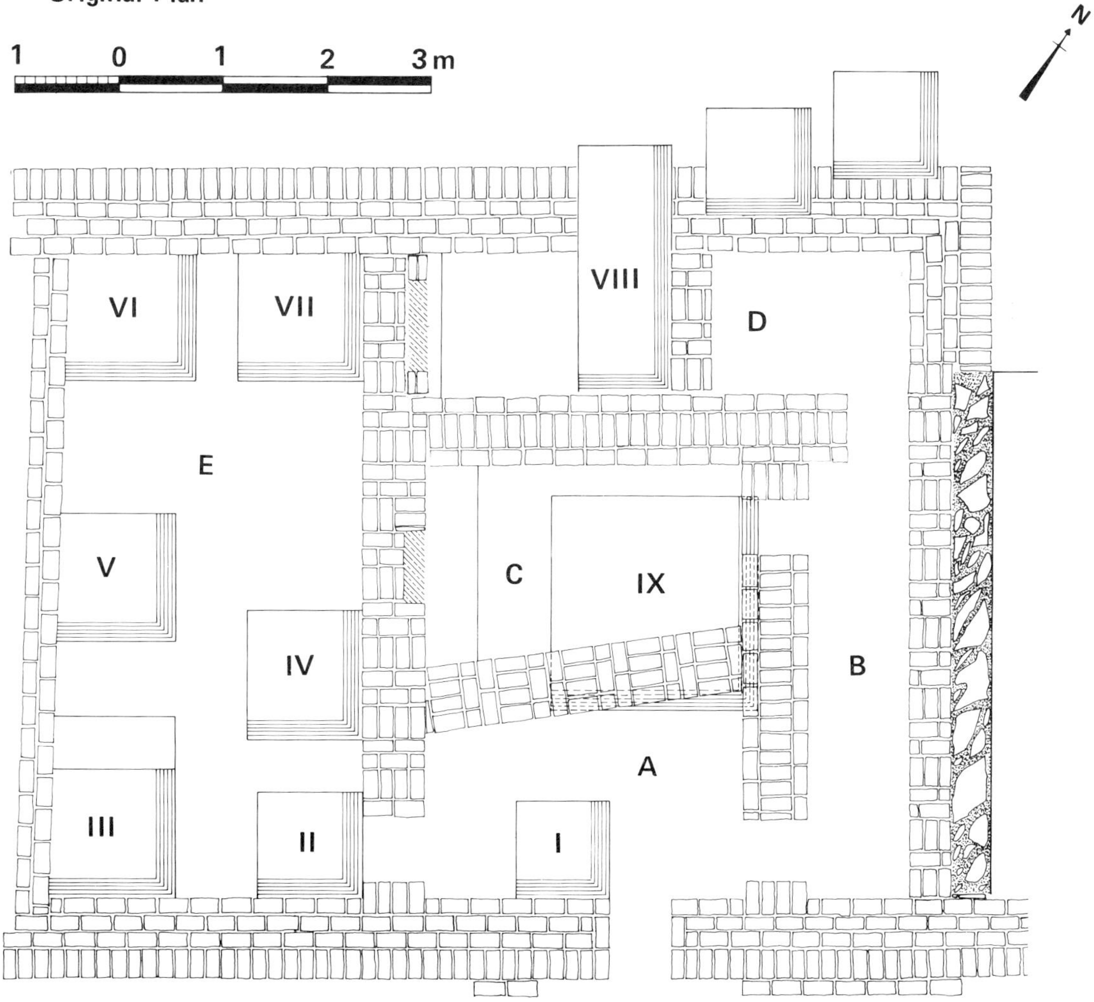

Plan with later additions

The Mastaba of Hesi

Plate 10

Hesi, false door

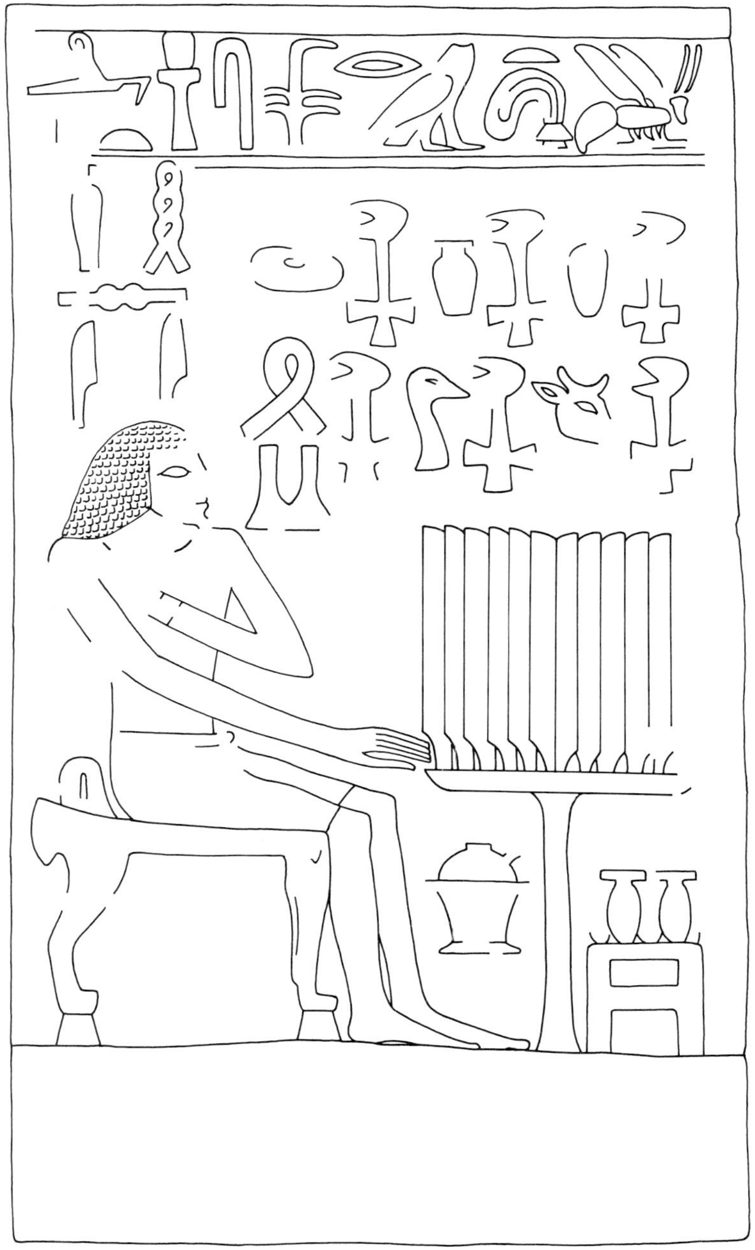

Hesi, panel of false door, detail

Plate 12

Hesi, chapel, false door of Tetiankh

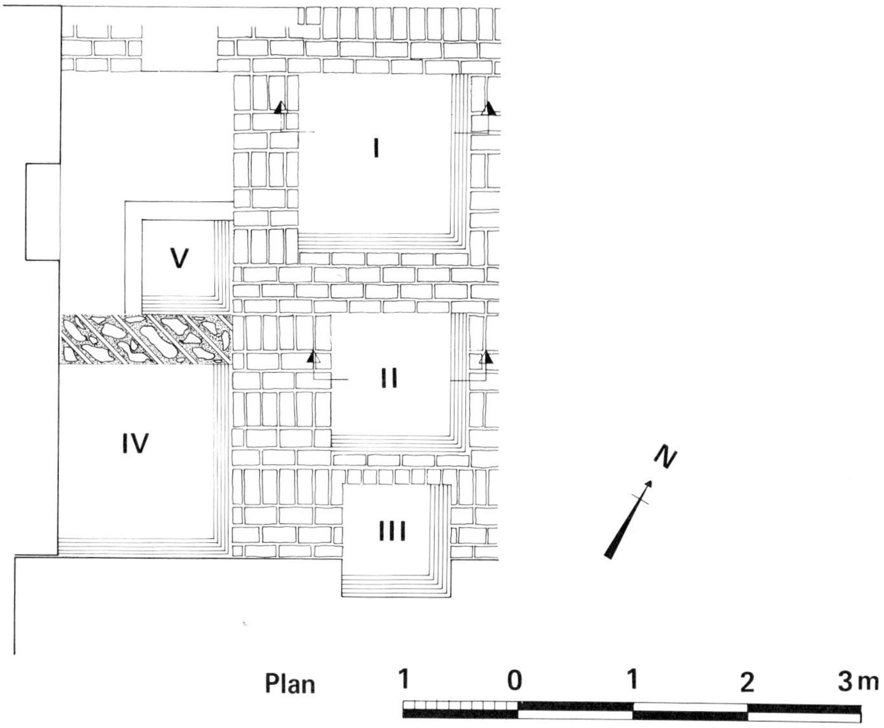

Plan

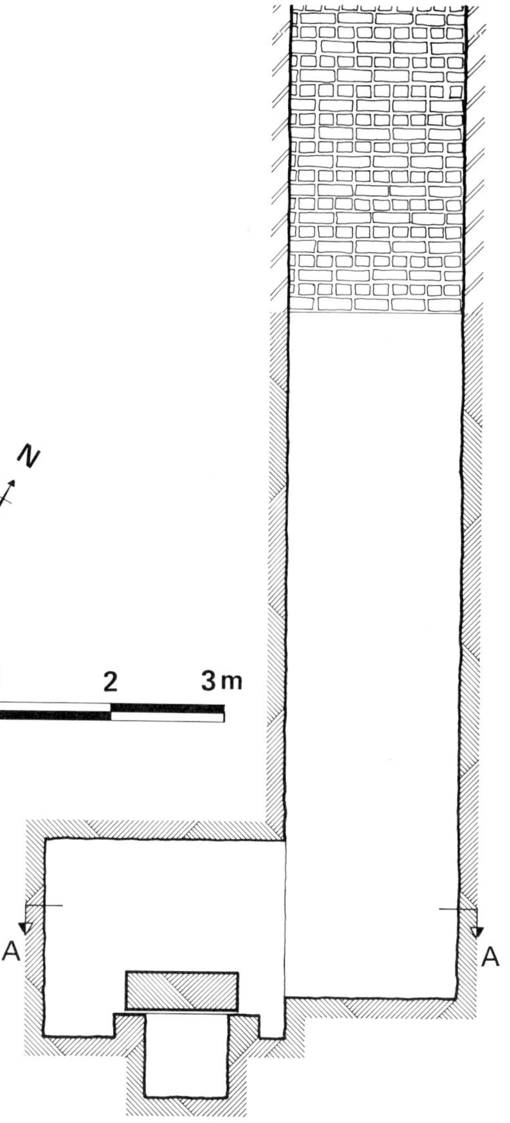

Shaft I

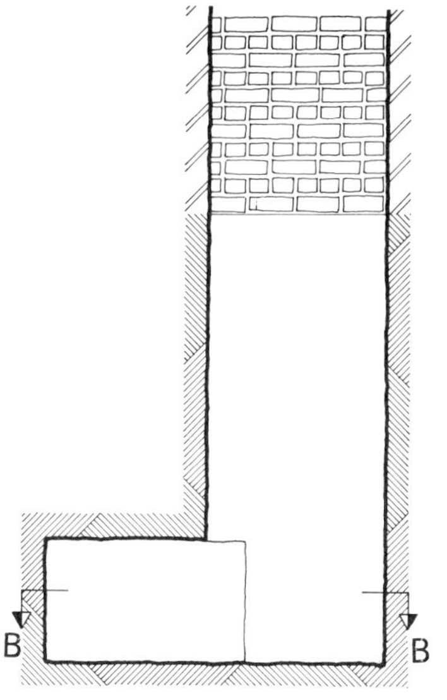

Shaft II

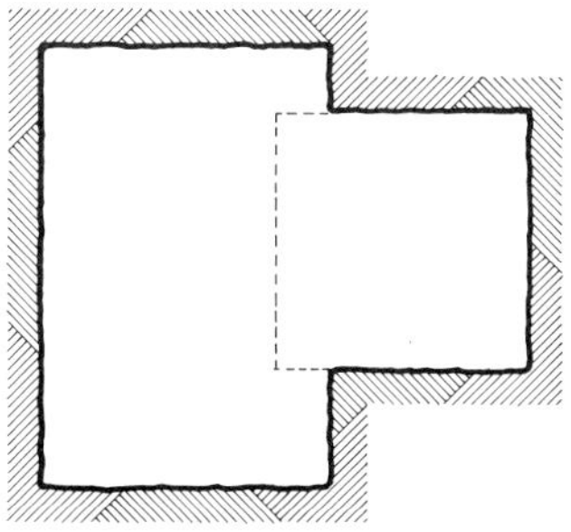
Section Plan B-B

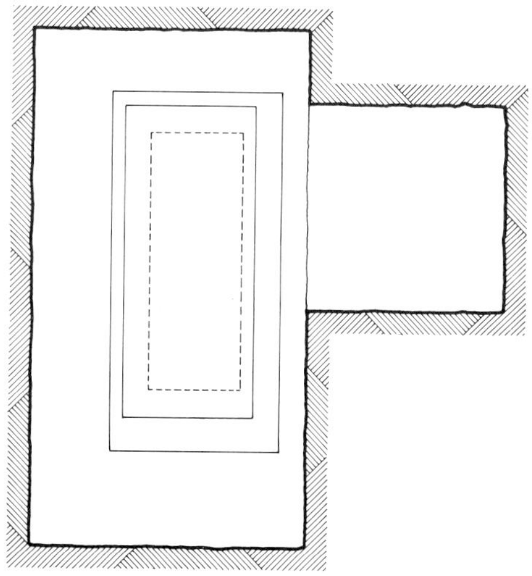
Section Plan A-A

Mastaba C

Plate 14

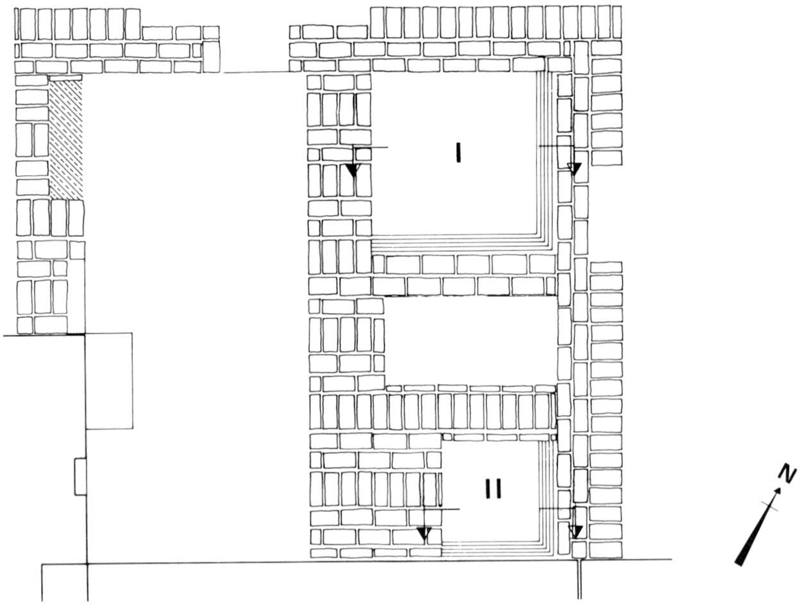

Original Plan

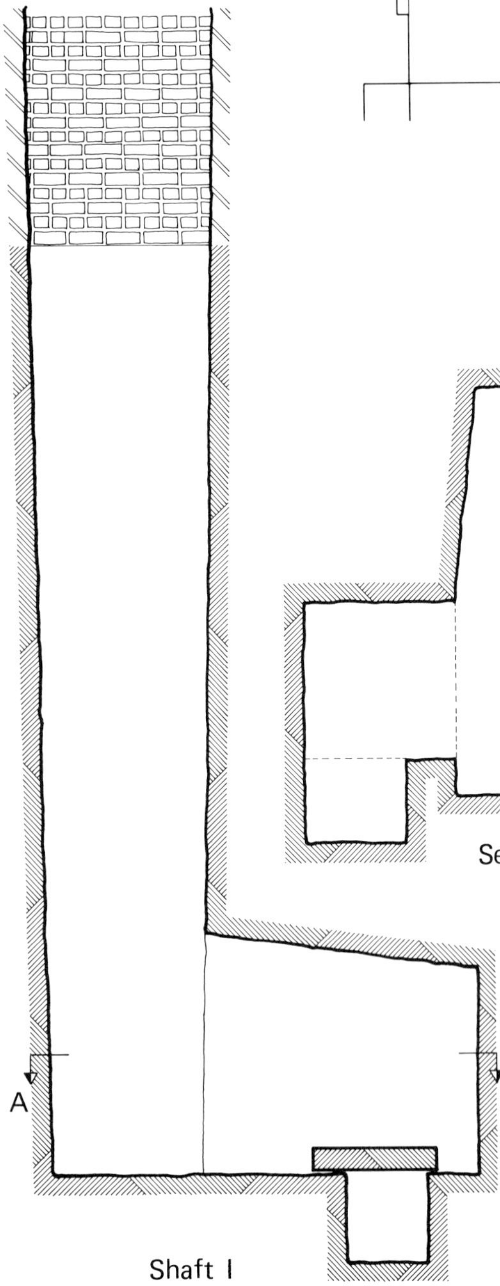

Shaft I

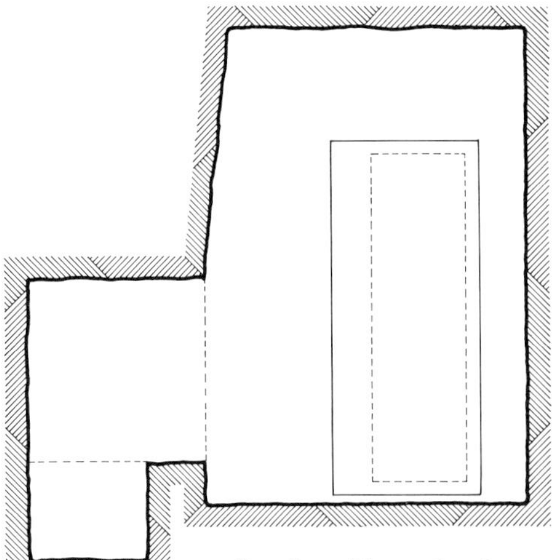

Section Plan A—A

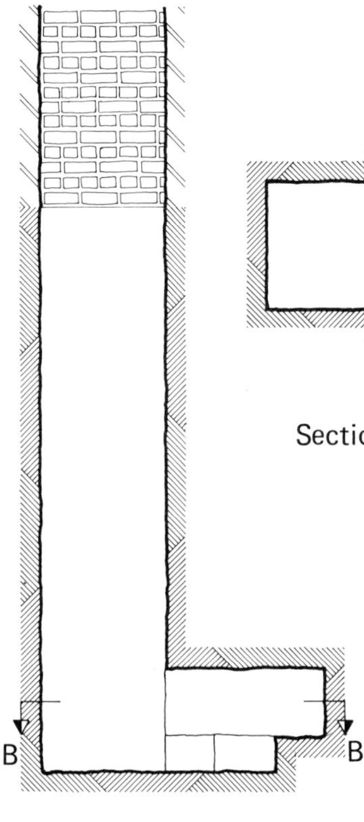

Shaft II

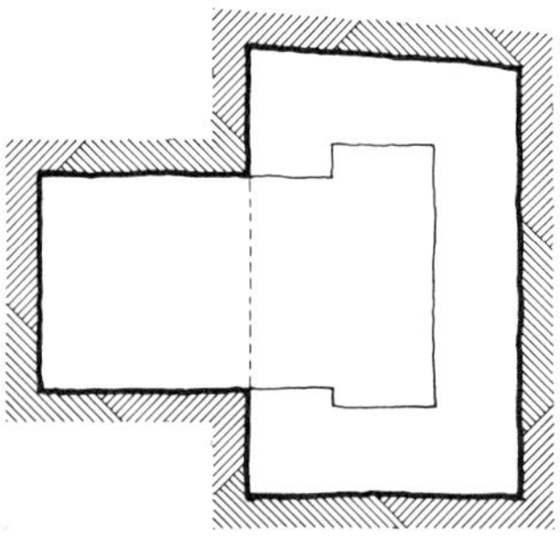

Section Plan B-B

The Mastaba of Ishfi

Plate 15

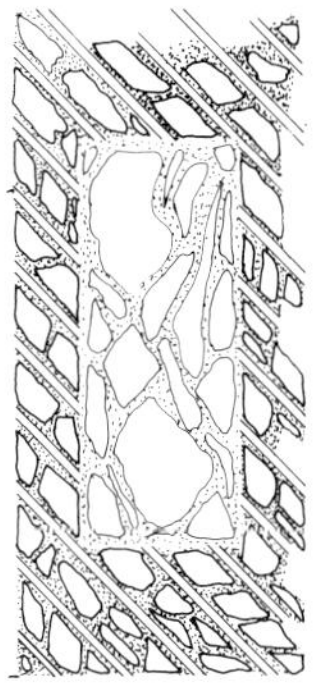

Wall over Shaft III

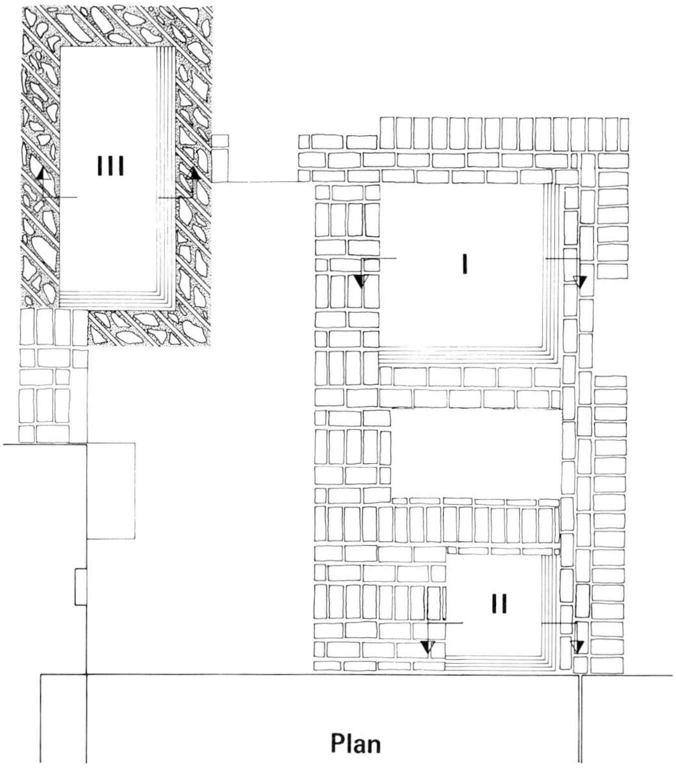

Plan

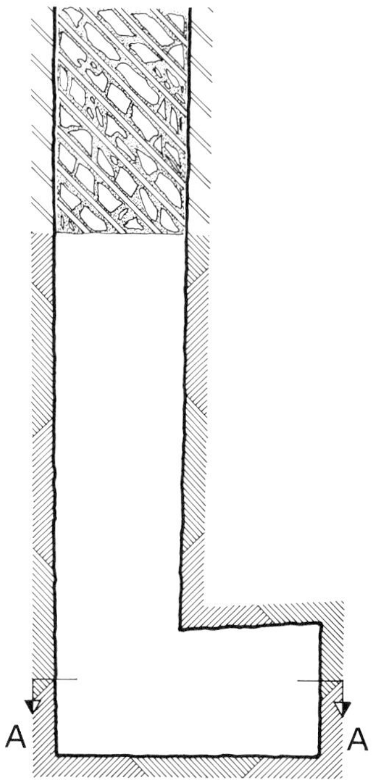

Section Plan A-A

Shaft III

The Mastaba of Ishfi: reuse by Mesi

Plate 16

Ishfi, lintel

Ishfi, false door

Ishfi, false door: upper section

Ishfi, false door: lower section

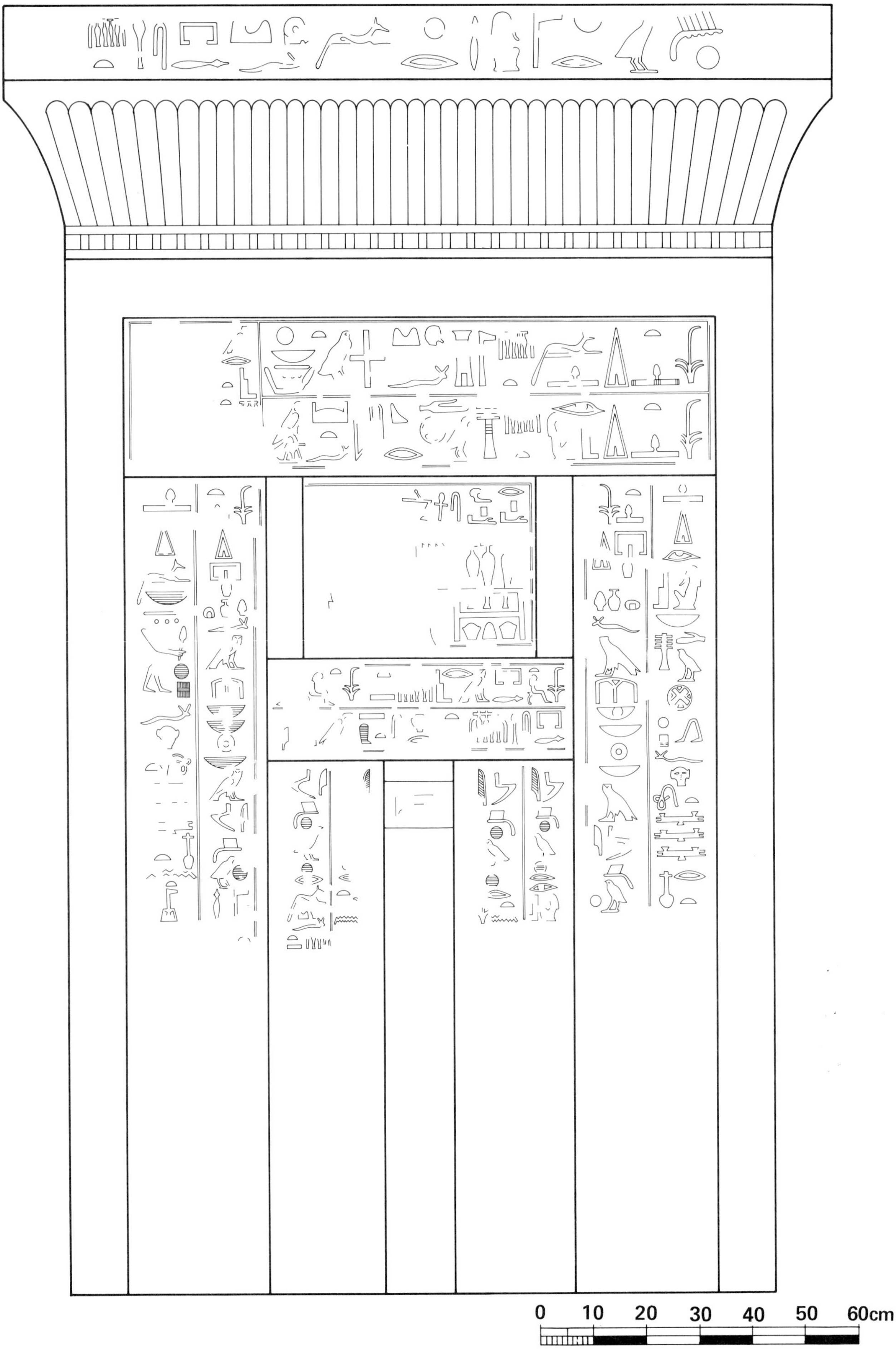

Ishfi: false door

Mesi, false door

Mesi, false door and side slab, reconstruction

Plate 20

Ked, false door
S88:FD 2

Mesi, side slab: detail

Plate 21

Kai, false door

S84:FD1

Khnumhetep, false door
S88:FD4

Hesut, false door
S88:FD3

Plate 23

Iri, offering basin S83:OT1

Kedut, offering table

S88:OT2

Kasedja, false door

S88:FD5

Plate 24

Kedet, offering table
S88:OT3

Pepyankh, obelisk
S84:178

Djefti, offering table
S88:OT4

S83:1

S83:9

Fragments

Plate 26

S83:22

S83:27

S83:26

Fragments

Plate 27

S83:24

S83:28

S83:30

S83:31

S83:29

S83:34

S83:35

Fragments

Plate 28

S83:46

S83:45

S83:38

S83:49

S83:59

S83:48

Fragments

Plate 29

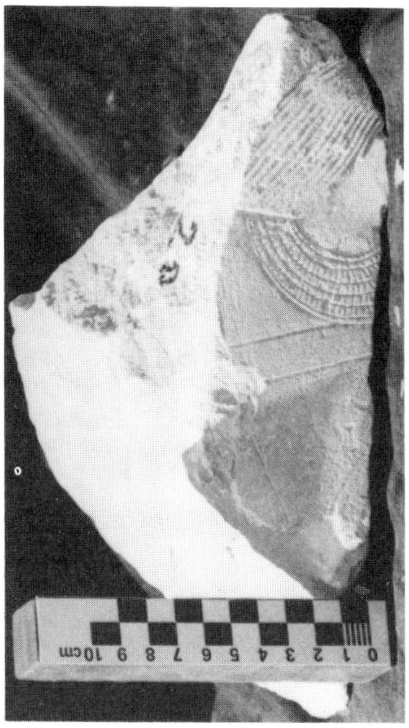

S83:60

S83:61

S83:63

S83:68

S83:74

S83:64

S83:80

S83:70

Fragments

Plate 30

S83:79

S83:86

S83:85

S83:103

S83:105

Fragments

S83:122

S84:163a

S83:127

S84:163c

S84:163b

Fragments

Plate 32

S84:157

S84:179

S84:164

S84:184

S84:183

Fragments

Plate 33

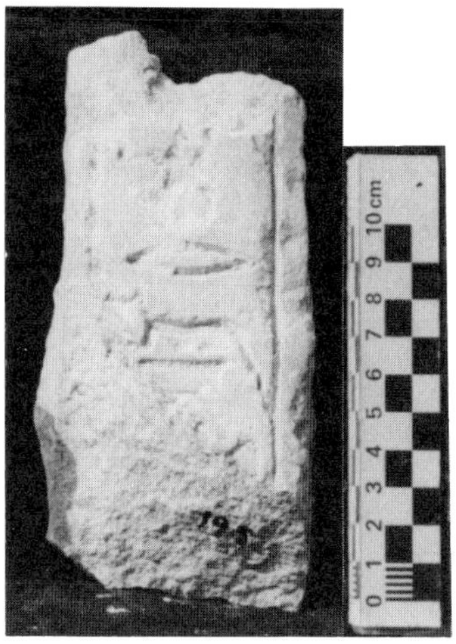

S84:195

S84:208

S84:205 a-e

S84:209

S84:211

Fragments

Plate 34

S84:212

S84:213

S84:227

S84:223

S84:222

Fragments

Plate 35

S84:238

S84:243

S84:251

Fragments

Plate 36

S84:241

S84:242

S84:246

Fragments

Plate 37

S84:249

S84:250

S84:253

S84:254

Fragments

Plate 38

S84:255

S84:256

S84:257

S84:259

S84:261

S84:263

Fragments

Plate 39

S84:262

S84:265

S84:270

S84:275

S88:2

Fragments

Plate 40

S88:1

S88:2

S88:16

S88:17

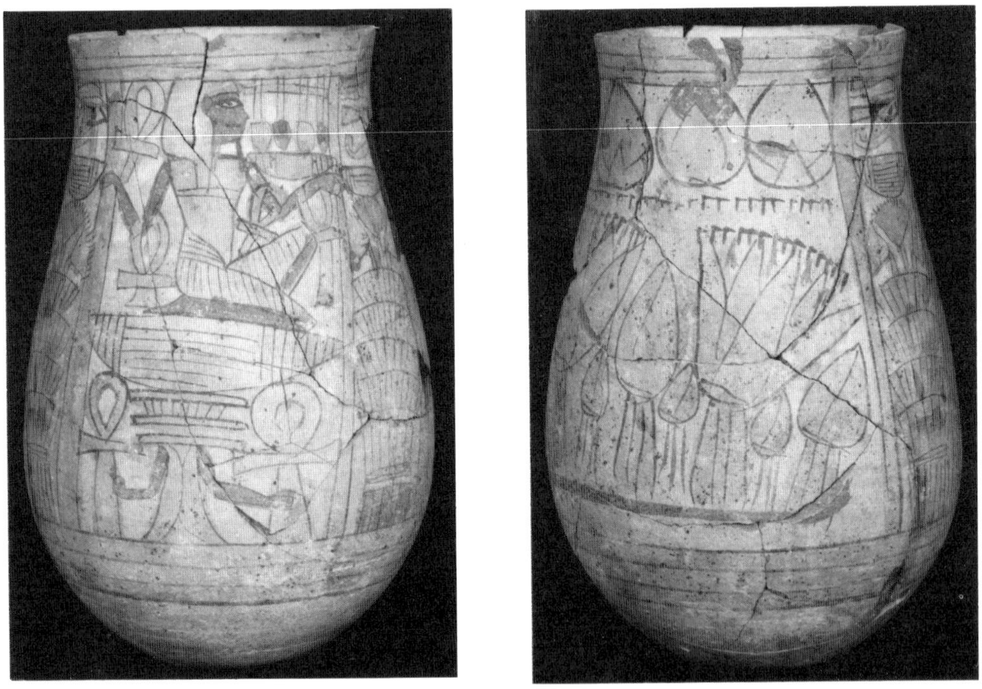
S88:9

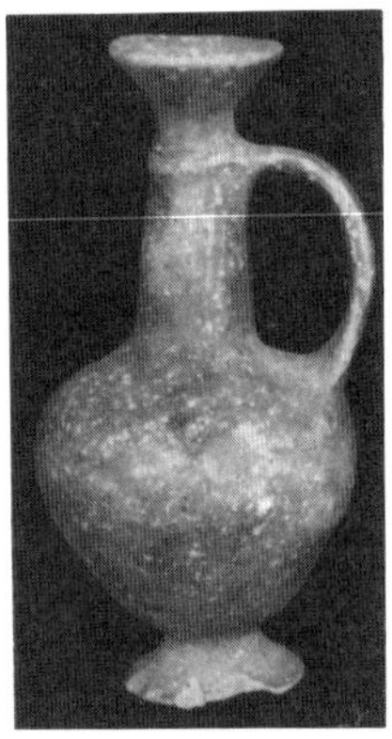
S88:22

S88:46

S88:67

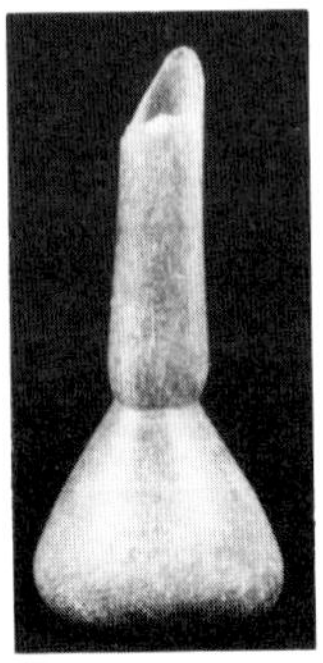
S88:69

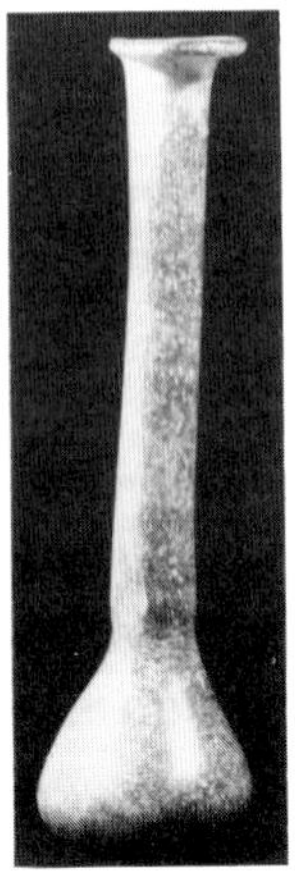
S88:25

Plate 41

S88:27

S88:29

S88:44

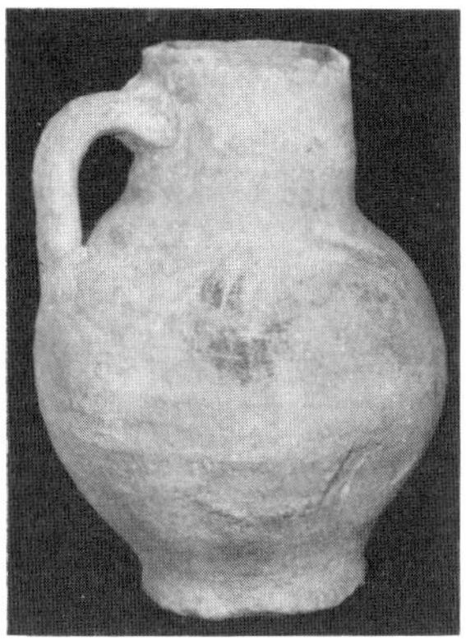

S88:28

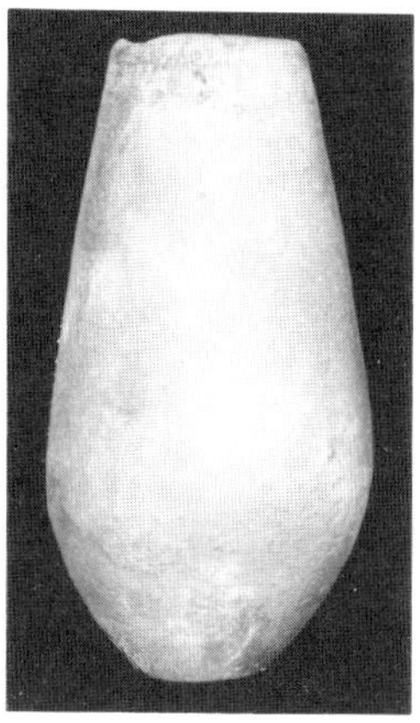

S88:32

S88:21

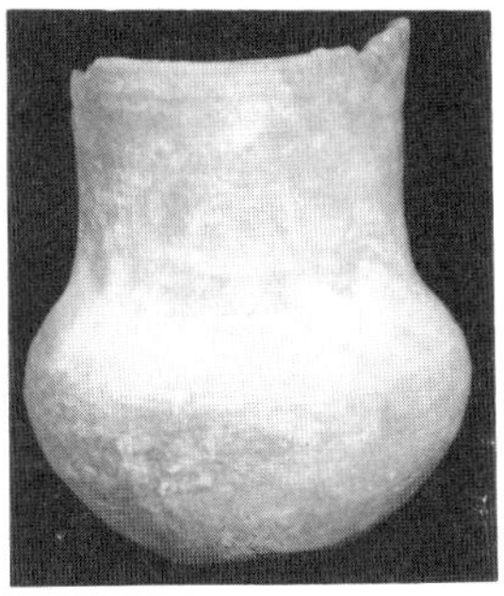

S88:36

S88:38

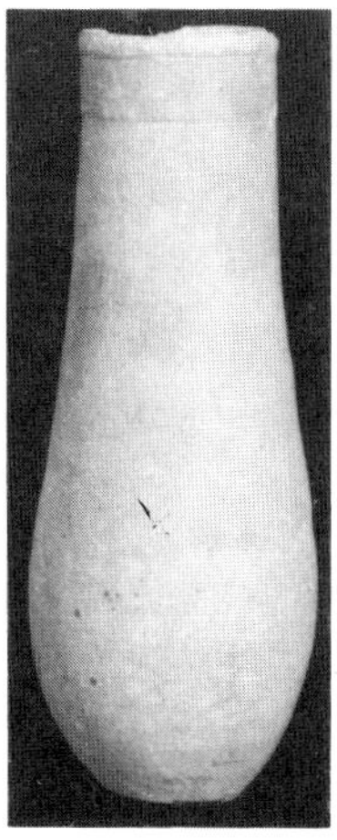

S88:49

S88:43

S88:52

S88:53

S88:45

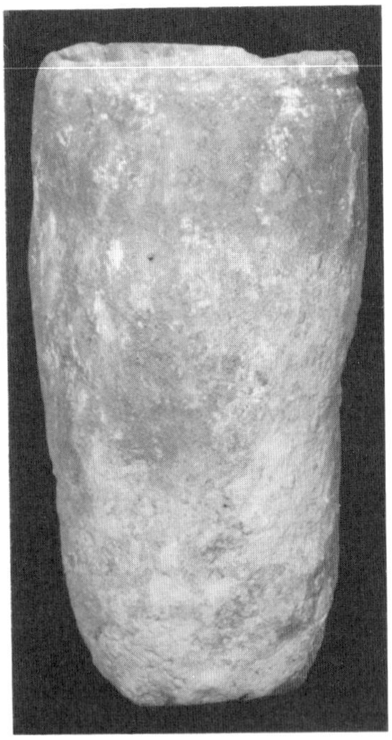

S88:57

S88:58

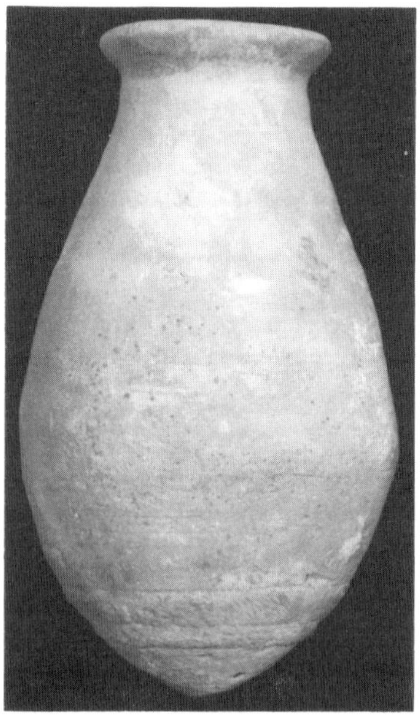

S88:54

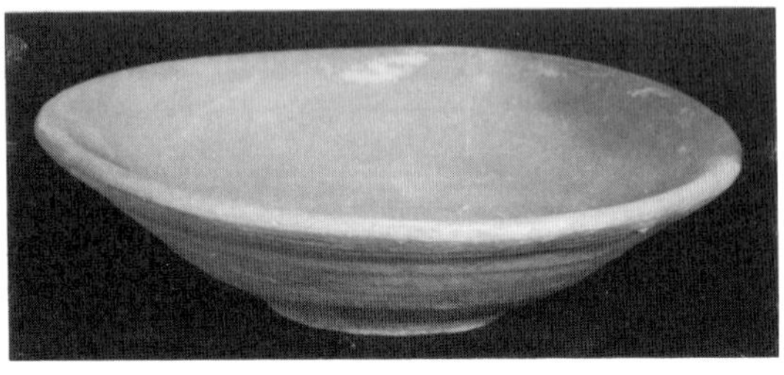

S88:66

S88:65

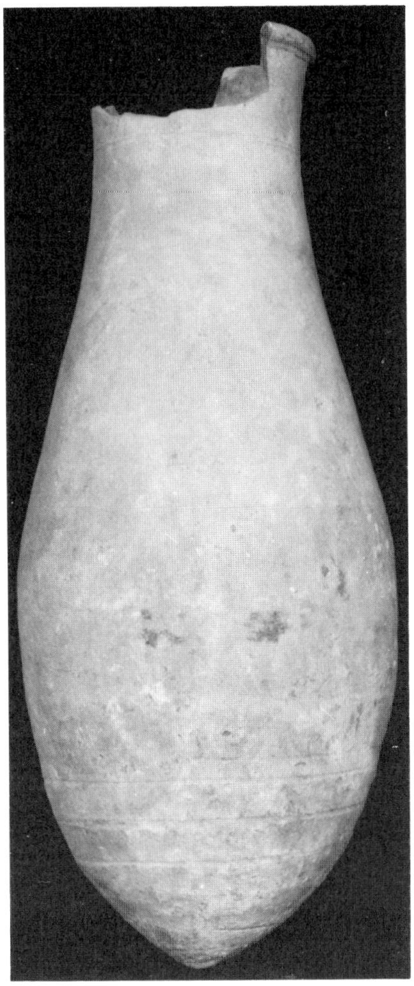

S88:59

S88:60

S88:64

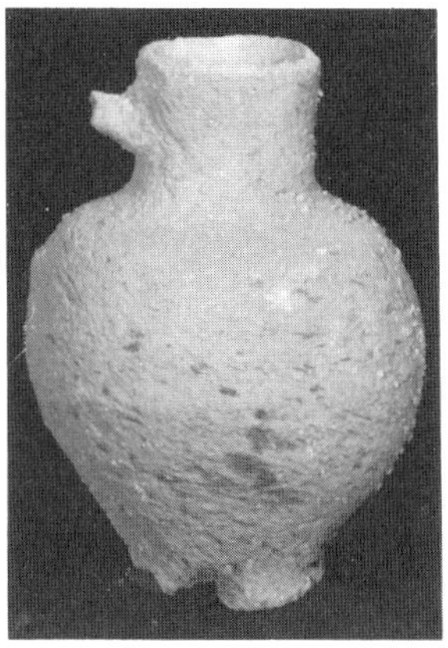

S88:70

S88:74

S88:61

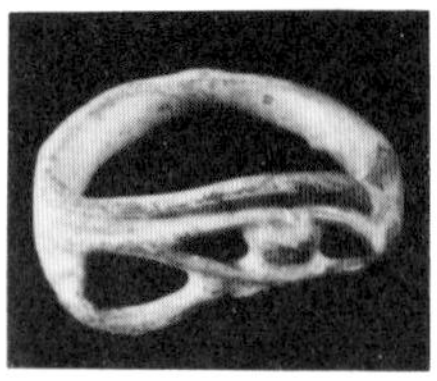
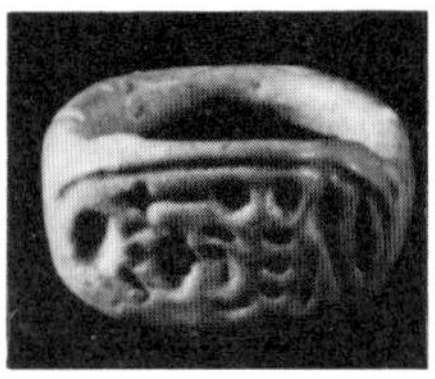
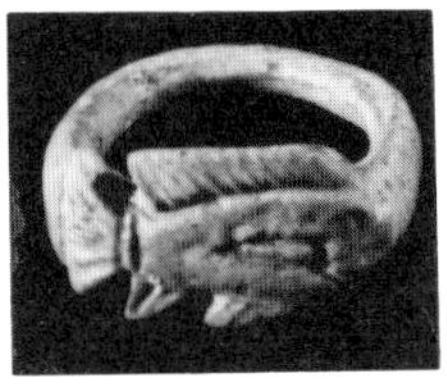
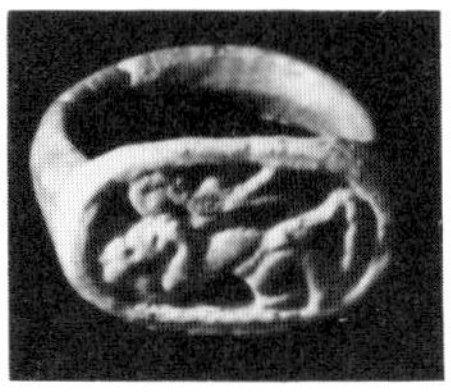

a b c d

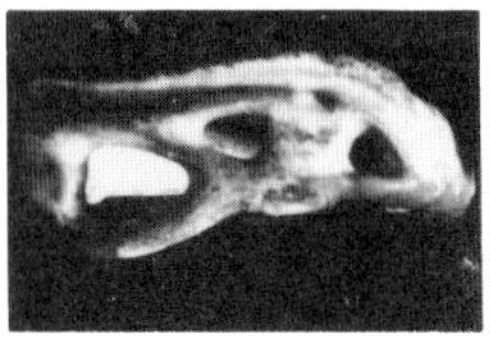
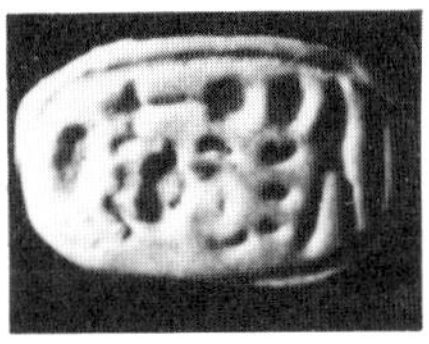

a b c d

S88:31 A

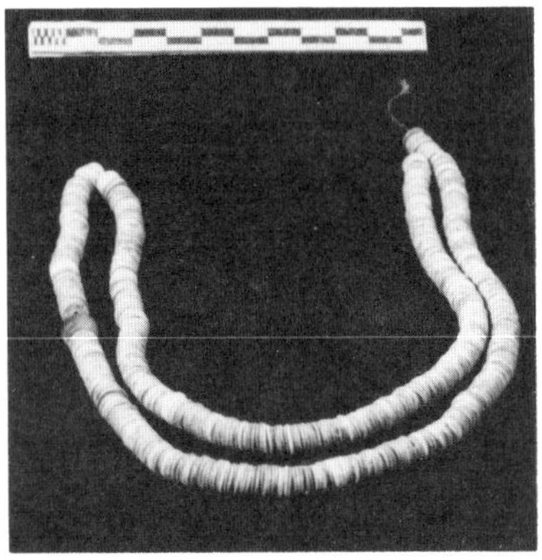

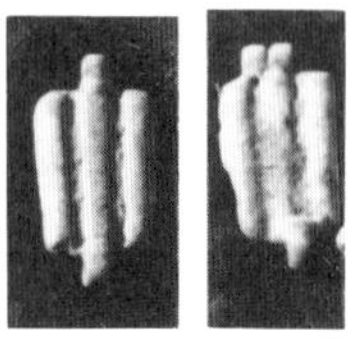
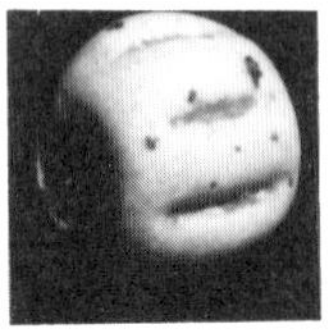

b c d

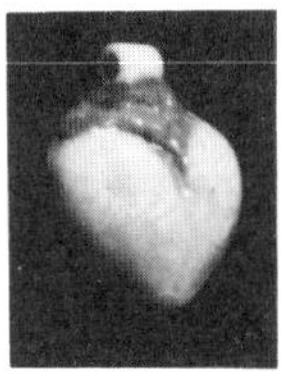

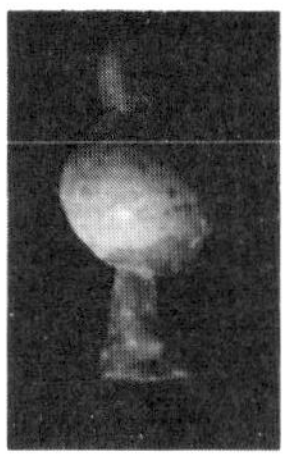

a f f f

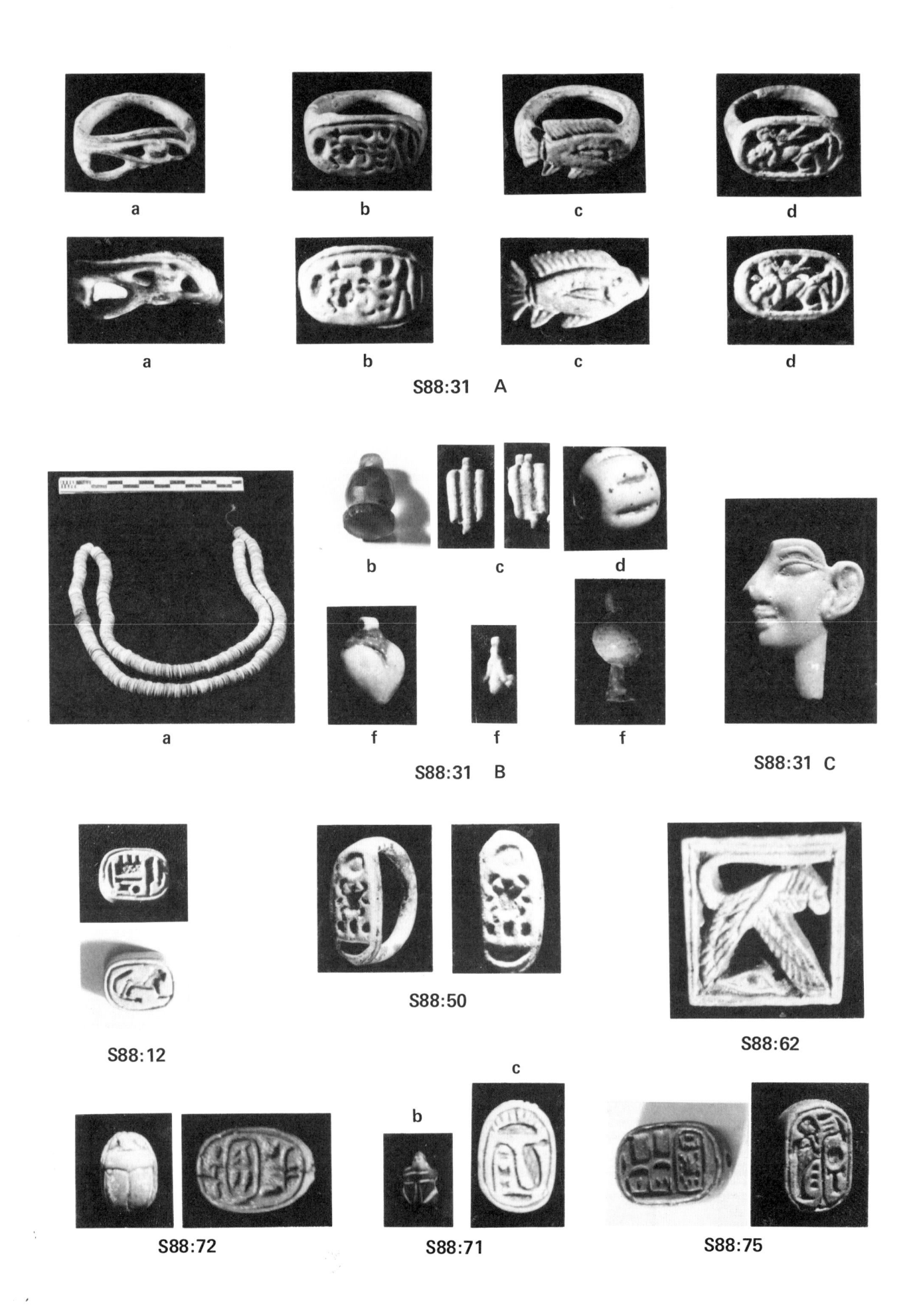

S88:31 B

S88:31 C

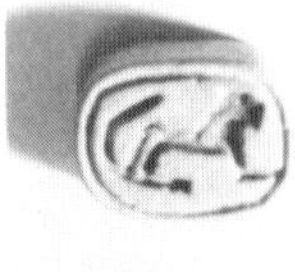

S88:12

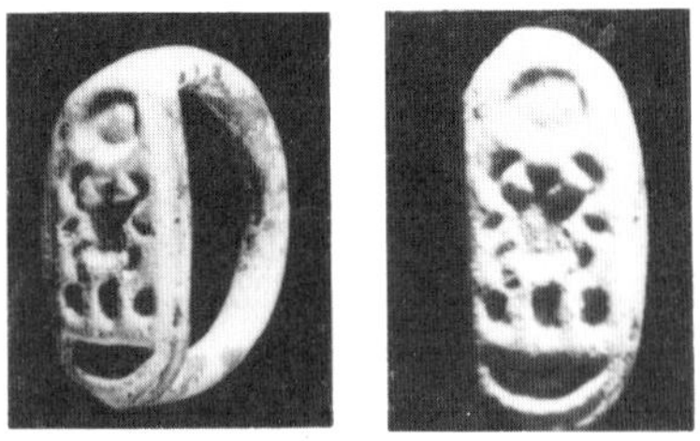

S88:50

S88:62

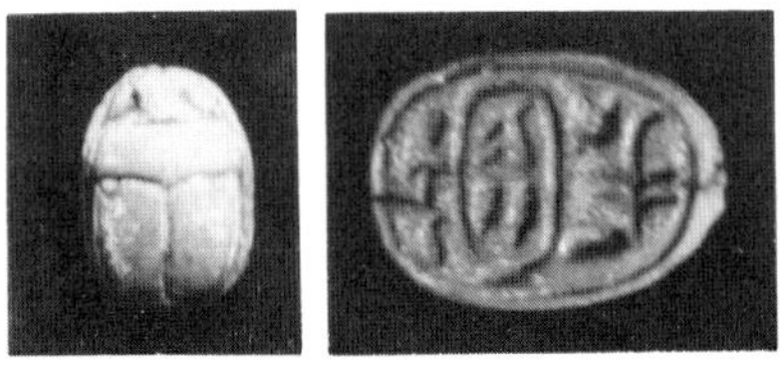

S88:72

b

c

S88:71

S88:75

b

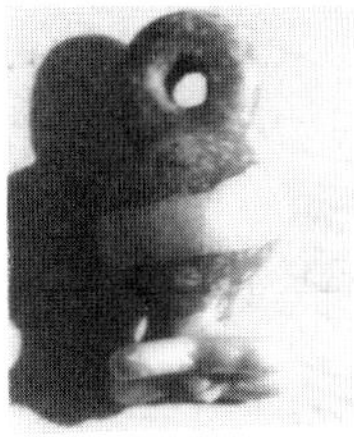

d

e

a

a

c

f

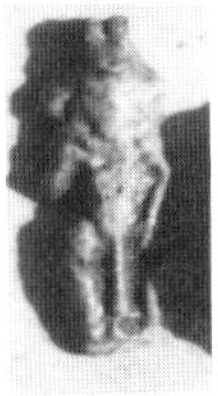

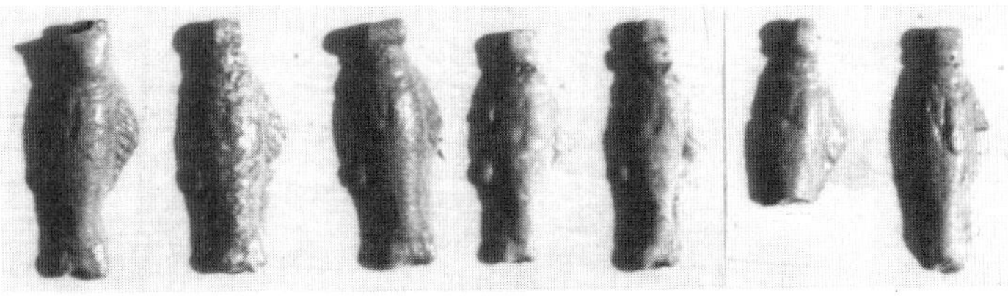

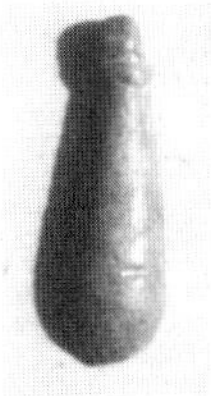

g

h

i

S88:76

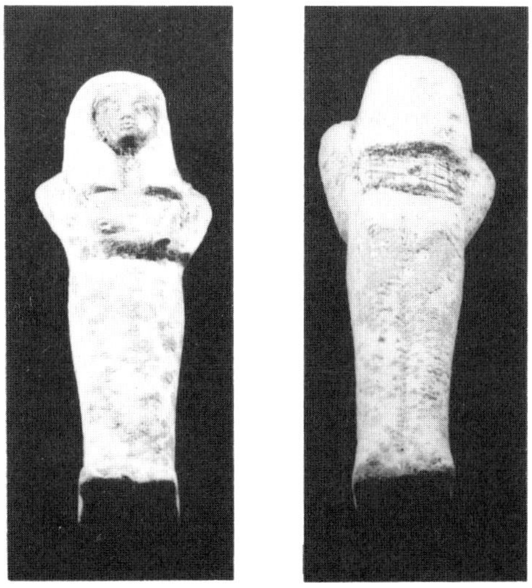

S88:24

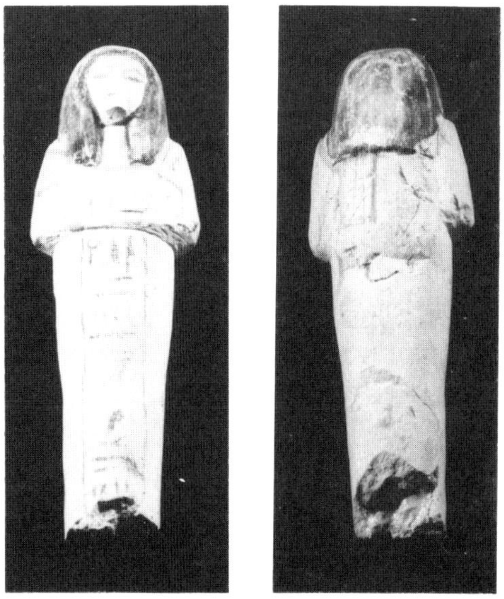

S88:40

Burial 2

Burial 10

Burial 9

Burial 12

S88:31A(b)

S88:50

S88:71(c)

S88:12

S88:40

S88:75

S88:76(c)

S88:76(b)

S88:72